BC 39810

813
HUT

Hutchinson, Stuart.

Henry James : an
American as
modernist.

Critical Studies Series

HENRY JAMES:
An American as Modernist

HENRY JAMES:
An American as Modernist

813
HUT

by
Stuart Hutchinson

VISION
and
BARNES & NOBLE

Vision Press Limited
11–14 Stanhope Mews West
London SW7 5RD

and

Barnes & Noble Books
81 Adams Drive
Totowa, NJ 07512

ISBN (UK) 0 85478 205 2
ISBN (US) 0 389 20344 0

Printed and bound in Great Britain by
Unwin Brothers Ltd.,
Old Woking, Surrey.
Phototypeset by Galleon Photosetting,
Ipswich, Suffolk.
MCMLXXXII

Contents

Acknowledgements

A version of the chapter on *The Wings of the Dove* first appeared in *Essays in Criticism*. I thank the editors for permission to reprint this material.

More personally, I thank my friend and colleague Keith Carabine for his generous and valuable help throughout the writing of this book.

Introduction

The major nineteenth-century American authors were necessarily modernists in the sense of being fabricators, rather than imitators, of reality. They belonged to a nation recently invented and still provisional. Unlike nineteenth-century English and European writers, they were unprovided with traditional structures of reality so long established in history as to seem impersonal and absolute. To import European structures, which American writers frequently did, only exposed these structures as artificial. They were revealed in America to have no more authoritative a claim on reality than any of the unregulated forms in which the new nation was creating itself. Indeed for nineteenth-century American writers as for the twentieth-century modernists all structures, all meanings, remained contrivances. Huck Finn, therefore, is made to enter his novel of irreconcilable fabrications by confessing his origin, not in a supposedly objective and real world, but in another book. Similarly, the protean *Ulysses* affirms by its dependence on Homer that form is always fiction.

Though James tried to, he could not escape implication in the inchoate energies of his nation. Like several of his characters, he came to Europe to find relief from personal and national self-creation uncheckable in America by any reference to authority. He wanted to find objectivity, and therefore completeness, for the self amid the traditions of Europe. As a novelist, he was ambitious to produce work which, in its realism, would rival that of the great English and European novelists. Like theirs, his realism would imitate structures of

7

life outside the novel: structures so validated by history as to seem part of the objective system of things.

The Europe he sought, however, was already passing away even as he arrived. As in America, so in Europe, reality was being revealed as the product of the form in which it was expressed. Every form was no more than one window in the construction of what remained, in James's famous phrase, 'a house of fiction'. The difference between America and Europe was that the former faced the creation of itself, the latter the recreation of itself. America was a mysterious blank stage, its new actors barely costumed by time. On the European stage, by contrast, there was hardly room to move amid structures from the past, while the guises in the wardrobe reached back to genesis.

Such is the American and European context in which I place James and the seven novels I deal with in this book. I begin with *Washington Square*, where James fakes tones of European urbanity, and end in the labyrinths of *The Golden Bowl*, where James is nearly as invisible as the later Joyce. Seven novels cannot of course tell the whole story of an author, the sheer mass of whose work, as Pound observed, was labour for two lifetimes. I hope, however, that I tell a significant part of the story, avoiding much of the repetitiousness endemic in the limitations of what any critic has to say.

1

Washington Square: The Look of a Social History

1

After the strange, unsettled territories of *The Prairie*, *The Narrative of Arthur Gordon Pym*, *The Scarlet Letter*, *Moby-Dick* and *Adventures of Huckleberry Finn*, *Washington Square* can seem, especially for English readers, to encompass more reassuring ground. For a start, the manner in which the novel is delivered to us by James suggests a great deal of confidence on his part. It's as if he is as untroubled as Jane Austen about the relationship between author and reader. Consequently, he can readily offer himself as a mediator between us and the novel's events. This kind of confident, authorial voice is rarely found in American novels before James. In Melville's case, for example, D. H. Lawrence diagnosed a split within *Moby-Dick* itself between the man, who 'was a real American in that he always felt his audience in front of him', and the artist, who only comes into his own, 'when he ceases to be American, when he forgets all audience'.[1] This diagnosis is significant enough in highlighting the fact that for nineteenth-century American writers the audience was certainly more of a burden than it was for their English counterparts. They *felt* it in front of them, because they could not be sure they were carrying it along. What assumptions could an American audience be relied on as having? The vast country was still to be settled, the national identity still to be created. What assumptions for that matter

9

could a nineteenth-century American writer have about himself? Uncertainty about audience mirrored uncertainty about authorial self. To what did one's authorial voice belong?

The effort to answer such questions is evident in the protean aspects of nineteenth-century American literature and (what amounts to the same thing) in the irreconcilability and furtiveness of its authorial voices, even within a single work. As we begin *Washington Square*, however, James seems to be unaware the questions exist. His relationship with his readers seems to be as easy as Jane Austen's with hers, because he apparently has the same kind of readers in mind. They constitute an audience with an established sense of itself. If they dwell in America, they might well be living in an imitative European style in such a place as Washington Square. The Square has 'a kind of established repose . . . the look, of having had something of a social history' (Ch. 3).[2] To this kind of audience the novel can be urbanely delivered in relation to shared standards and values. Though *Washington Square* will have some peculiar American ingredients, it will by and large (so the author's manner implies) present the kind of characters and events readers will be long familiar with. It will deal with the expectations of parents and children, with the passing on of wealth and property, and, inevitably, with marriage.

And yet by the time *Washington Square* was published, Dickens and George Eliot, in *Great Expectations* and *Daniel Deronda* for example, had already registered their own loss of faith in English civilization's confident possession of the world. Entailed by this loss was a corresponding diminution of that common understanding formally shared between author and reader. The revelations of the plot in *Great Expectations* tell us everything and nothing, while very few readers of *Daniel Deronda* are carried along by Daniel's Zionist mission. What right then has James, given the uncertainties of the American *and* English novelists who precede him, to his apparent confidence? The answer is none at all. That is the point. The manner of the telling of *Washington Square* is after all strikingly affected. It is *adopted* by James to solve the kind of problems to do with authorial self and audience that the major American writers found irresolvable. For James, it serves the same purpose as does Washington Square for the people living there. It lays claim to participation in a civilized and established order of things. Neither for James, nor for those confined in the Square, however, has the claim any validity beyond itself. This is why James's authorial voice, unlike Jane Austen's, and that of early Dickens and George Eliot, is not felt to be part of any sustaining life going on outside the novel. It's why also Washington Square has only the *look* of a social history. In this novel, author and characters may do no more than pretend to an authoritative possession of the world. In fact, James's authorial manner in *Washington Square* is as much a matter of creative self-display, and even of self-idealization, as are any of Whitman's voices in 'Song of Myself', Melville's in *Moby-Dick*, or Twain's in *Huckleberry Finn*.

In its self-consciousness about its form as a novel, *Washington Square* is revealed after all to be very much an American work. In this respect, too, it is revealed to be incipiently modernist. For author and characters, expectations of order have no guarantee of fulfilment and may indeed have no validity beyond the purpose for which they are assumed. As they live with this fate, James's characters are surrogates for himself. Unlike him, however, they remain unconsoled by intercourse with a lover (the reader!) fashioned to their own design.

2

Dr. Sloper, to begin where James begins, is revealed to have had unexceptional expectations. He has wanted to be conscientious and successful in his chosen profession. He has wanted an 'amiable, graceful, accomplished, elegant' and 'pretty' (Ch. 1) wife, whose possession of ten thousand a year is certainly not a disadvantage. Finally, he has wanted a son. These expectations signify the world Dr. Sloper would like to believe in. It would be a world in which personal desire would find public fulfilment as expressed in one's profession, one's marriage, and one's family. The world would respond compliantly, even approvingly, to one's design on it. Such 'civilized' assumptions are recognizably congruent with those James's authorial voice affects to believe in. From this perspective, then, the defeat of Dr. Sloper enacts and confirms the

11

defeat of James himself in his expectations of being a certain kind of novelist.

The Doctor is for James a representative figure. He is a representative American in his isolation from a sustaining community. In New York he is a 'local celebrity' (Ch. 1), but New York at this time, so James reveals, is a very small pond to be a big fish in. In New York Dr. Sloper has no equal. There is no one with the authority either to confirm or challenge his eminence. Following the Doctor's loss of his son and wife, James writes:

> Our friend . . . escaped criticism: that is, he escaped all criticism but his own, which was much the most competent and most formidable. He walked under the weight of this very private censure for the rest of his days, and bore forever the scars of a castigation to which the strongest hand he knew had treated him on the night that followed his wife's death. (Ch. 1)

To be so complete unto oneself can be reassuring, and certainly the Doctor has a confident manner. Yet the passage also indicates that to be unrelieved of a self like the Doctor's is a punishing burden. The Doctor's irony, in which his apparent self-confidence mainly finds expression, is like James's authorial manner very much of a performance. Intended in the Doctor's case to demonstrate his personal supremacy to all contingencies, it is essentially the irony of self-despair. In this respect it contrasts markedly with Mr. Bennet's in *Pride and Prejudice*. The two men share a resemblance in their misogyny, and in their enjoyment of the masculine privacy of their libraries. Mr. Bennet's irony, however, remains the irony of gratification. He has five daughters and no son. His wife is less intelligent than a wife of his should have been. Nonetheless, the world by and large answers to his design on it. His selfhood is not too challenged by the world, which remains ordered for his benefit by traditions so deeply implanted that their authority seems impersonal. Dr. Sloper by contrast, when it most matters to him, finds his sense of self and his sense of his world fundamentally undermined. Moreover, he lives in a country without upholding, impersonal traditions. As the second sentence of the novel reminds us, to be anything in America is only 'to put forward a claim'. It's to have only recently, as the Doctor has done, built one's house. The Doctor's claim, like that of many previous characters in American literature, is thrown back in his face. His house establishes no dominion.

His life in consequence becomes so poisoned that, in Mrs. Penniman's words, even his 'pleasures make one shudder' (Ch. 30). Here is his case against Morris Townsend, as he expresses it to the young man's sister.

> 'You women are all the same! But the type to which your brother belongs was made to be the ruin of you, and you were made to be its handmaids and victims. The sign of the type in question is the determination—sometimes terrible in its quiet intensity—to accept nothing of life but its pleasures, and to secure these pleasures chiefly by the aid of your complacent sex. Young men of this class never do anything for themselves that they can get other people to do for them, and it is the infatuation, the devotion, the superstition of others, that keeps them going. These other in ninety-nine cases out of a hundred are women. What our young friends chiefly insist upon is that someone else shall suffer for them; and women do that sort of thing, as you must know, wonderfully well.' The Doctor paused a moment, and then he added abruptly, 'You have suffered immensely for your brother!' (Ch. 14)

Throughout the chapter the Doctor derives great satisfaction from destroying Morris in his sister's eyes. He overwhelms Mrs. Montgomery. Till now, she has put up with Morris. He *is* her brother. During his conversation with her, however, the Doctor creates the terms for her sense of grievance against Morris, and even the grievance itself. The Doctor hates Morris, because he is the embodiment of everything the Doctor cannot be. Morris's very existence as a human being acts as a criticism of what the Doctor sees as the conscientiousness, rigour and self-denial by which he has conducted his own life. Morris, in the apparent easiness of his existence, reinforces the Doctor's despairing suspicion that the manner of *his* life has caused common gratifications to pass him by. In fact, in his one attempt to find a place in Morris's kind of world he has been rejected and humiliated. His wife was of Morris's world in the sense that she was to bring to the Doctor what Morris would bring to Catherine. His wife was, as Morris is to his daughter, beautiful to him. He married her 'for love'; for

13

relief from the burden of himself. As James states, with an ironic inclusiveness of reference which attests to the relativity of these things, she had 'the most charming eyes in the island of Manhattan' (Ch. 1). Marriage to her put within his grasp much of which he was deprived and is now still deprived—some of life's easy, shared pleasures and fulfilments. Convinced by his wife's death, however, that he betrayed a weakness in even desiring these things, and that so to expose oneself is inevitably to be hurt, he feels that to disapprove of Morris as a husband for Catherine is legitimately to protect her. He can imagine sympathetically that 'it must be deucedly pleasant for [Catherine] to have a beautiful young fellow to come and sit down beside her' (Ch. 9). But Catherine must not succumb to her temptation. She must not concede to what the Doctor sees as unreason, as 'infatuation' and 'superstition'. Morris, exploiting these weaknesses, has, in the Doctor's words, 'the assurance of the devil himself' (Ch. 7). In the Manicheism which it has been necessary for the Doctor to adopt so as to keep his bearings, all evil is visibly personified in the figure of his daughter's suitor. So much so, that he would 'have liked to kill him' (Ch. 32).

Clearly, from James's encompassing point of view, the Doctor's responses to Morris tell us as much about the Doctor himself as about Morris. They certainly tell us more about the Doctor than the Doctor himself knows. Morris, according to the Doctor, is an exploiter of women. But then so is the Doctor. He has housed Mrs. Penniman all these years, so that he can score easy victories over her. He asks her to make 'a clever woman' (Ch. 2) of his daughter, only because he despairs of her success and wants his misogyny confirmed. If Morris insists that someone else, especially a woman, shall suffer for him, then so does Dr. Sloper. No one in the book more causes a woman, his own daughter Catherine, to suffer than he does. No 'determination' could be more 'terrible in its quiet intensity' than his towards her. Deep down he even envies Morris's easy capacity to take and give pleasure. He half wishes he could relax his own guard against Morris's charm. If only *he* were being wooed again by someone beautiful and young—even a man. No wonder he tells Morris, 'I don't want to believe in you' (Ch. 12). To credit Morris is to

14

lose all self-possession, all the jealously guarded confines of identity.

It might reasonably be claimed that, before James, no American writer had managed a characterization as firm and developed as is the Doctor's. At the same time it must be recognized that characterization in a novel has everything to do with the structure of reality into which the characters are made to fit. Characterization was a problem for earlier American writers, because their world was so unprecedented. Unlike the contemporary English world, it was unfurnished with structures of reality which were the common possession of writers and readers, and which provided for imitative structures of realism in literature. Few, if any, characters in nineteenth-century American novels are confident of what they should be and do. The novels they are in are correspondingly provisional in structure. The characters feel themselves, and are represented as, the actors of uncertain roles. Frequently, they and their creators turn to moral allegory in an attempt to resolve fundamental self-doubt. Hunters, Indians, whales and (naturally) women are simply seen as either good or bad.

James, by contrast, appears to be mining an established seam with the characterization of Dr. Sloper. Both writer and reader might commonly assume a great many things about an intelligent, wealthy, widowed doctor, living with a marriageable daughter and a widowed sister in a fine house, in a society where the marrying of daughters is very much in the air, and where an impecunious suitor is in the offing. Immediately, the bare ingredients of the story begin to typify and structure themselves. Nearly all previous English novels are about marriage. A novelist, therefore, has a lot to build on, especially if, even in America, he has a setting so like an English setting. as is Washington Square.

And yet what greater right to his assumptions about the Doctor does James have, than the Doctor has to his assumptions about Morris? Within the Doctor's own idea of order his characterization of Morris undoubtedly has that 'solidity of specification' which James, in 'The Art of Fiction' (1884), was soon to claim to be 'the supreme virtue of a novel'. In criticizing the Doctor's account of Morris and of everything else, therefore, James is also turning a critical eye on how he himself composes. The imported structure James imposes on *Washington Square*, from which its solidity of specification and developed characterization derive, is no more absolute and no less artificial than the structure the Doctor imposes within *Washington Square*. This is why we can never be sure the Doctor isn't right about Morris. Furthermore, if the Doctor feels devastated when deprived of *his* idea of order, what reprieve from a similar fate can James himself claim? What more than Dr. Sloper has James himself to say in that 'lonely valley of the Alps', amid 'the hard featured rocks and glowing sky', the place 'so desolate and lonely', 'ugly and lonely' (Ch. 24)?

It is appropriate that this scene in the Alps should remind us both of 'The Whiteness of the Whale' in *Moby-Dick*, and also of Chapter 1 of Book 2 in *Little Dorrit*, when the 'fellow travellers' 'in the autumn of the year' pass through the 'Great Saint Bernard' as 'Darkness and Night [are] creeping up to the highest ridges of the Alps.' James is at the meeting point of American and European cultures at the end of the nineteenth century. In the chapter from *Moby-Dick* we have the inescapable American sense that the blankness of reality offers no recognition and escapes every human structure. In *Little Dorrit* we experience the beginning of the end of English civilization's confident possession of the world in its own image. Between the heat at the beginning of Book 1 in *Little Dorrit* and the cold at the beginning of Book 2, we live in a place that is not our own. Such too is the Doctor's knowledge in the Alps, when the desolation around him mirrors his sense of the desolation within his own heart. 'I am not a very good man', he tells Catherine. Now his representative American fate of isolation, and of dispossession of ideals which must have seemed so graspable, becomes a representative modern fate.

Catherine's story is eventually the same as her father's. Her mother, after whom she is named, died a week after her birth. Her father therefore needs her 'filial passion' (Ch. 2) as compensation for the love he lost with the death of his wife, and as consolation for the death of his son. He has no one else on whom to bestow his considerable, if restrained, fund of tenderness. Until Morris appears, Catherine has long accustomed him to having no rivals for her love and admiration. In fact

16

one of the ways James places the Doctor is by inviting us to take a more critical view of him than Catherine is capable of. The young girl is dazzled by her father: his 'great faculties seemed, as they stretched away, to lose themselves in a sort of luminous vagueness, which indicated, not that they stopped, but that Catherine's own mind ceased to follow them' (Ch. 2).

For James the Doctor's faculties do stop. Even though Catherine is to grow in the story and break with her father, however, her sense of life is finally confirmed as his. To Morris, she says of her father:

> He can't help it; we can't govern our affections. Do I govern mine? Mightn't he say that to me? It's because he is so fond of my mother, whom he lost so long ago. She was beautiful, and very, very, brilliant; he is always thinking of her. I am not at all like her. (Ch. 26)

Catherine *is* like her father. She wants to marry, as he did, to bring beauty into her life. Even on the verge of marriage, however, she is resigned to her father's sense that the passions and affections betray and expose one. In the Alps, Dr. Sloper's confession that he was 'not a very good man' was related to his assertion that 'at bottom I am very passionate.' Here with Morris, Catherine's understanding of her own 'affections' is of something ungovernable and rebellious, something not to be mediated by any system of manners and allegiances. Not even in Washington Square, a sort of island of tradition in New York and America, do structures of order help with the accommodation of real needs. Not even there does personal desire find harmonious public expression. We are reminded again that Washington Square has only 'the look' of what society in a Jane Austen novel has for real. Its order, only recently established, is manifestly no less of a contrivance or affectation than any other system. What right has it to govern the will and affections? On what authority can it promise to fulfil?

Like her father, Catherine feels very much thrust in on herself. In a relationship with Morris, she seeks recognition, accommodation, *love*, from someone other than herself. Her marriage would be a sign that life is hospitable to her deepest needs. It would be a sign of a coherence on terms inclusive of,

17

but greater than, the entirely personal. Morris's desertion of her, therefore, confirms her fundamental sense of dispossession. She has sought a fulfilling intercourse with life and been rejected and humiliated. She will never risk herself again—not even when John Ludlow, apparently a most suitable candidate, is ready to marry her. Her life now is barren, but it is contained. It expects nothing.

Her reductiveness, which is a numbing proclamation of a kind of order, is hardly disturbed even by Morris's reappearance in the final chapter:

> It seemed to be he, and yet not he; it was the man who had been everything, and yet this person was nothing. How long ago it was—how old she had grown—how much she had lived! She had lived on something that was connected with *him*, and she had consumed it in doing so. This person did not look unhappy. He was fair and well-preserved, perfectly dressed, mature and complete. As Catherine looked at him, the story of his life defined itself in his eyes: he had made himself comfortable, and he had never been caught.

Both Catherine and Morris have desired from each other more than a relationship can be expected to give. Each transforms the other into a figure of absolute value, because neither of their lives is part of anything else that sustains and fulfills. Catherine's surprise at the change Morris has undergone is in part natural, but it is also a criticism of the terms on which she desired to possess him. The former 'beautiful young man' was to have been 'her own exclusive property' (Ch. 26).

If Morris had married Catherine *with* her father's money, perhaps, as Mrs. Almond suggests, he could have performed the role Catherine demands of him. And yet to have allowed himself to be so completely possessed! Was not Catherine asking too much of him, just as Gatsby out of an equal dispossession was asking too much of Daisy? How could Morris have let himself be so 'consumed'? He must live and change on his own behalf. Catherine, however, has so much at stake on *her* Morris, that she is taken aback by the man she now sees. She imagines she has lived much, but sadly she has hardly lived at all. Almost any amount of life would have enabled her to see Morris in perspective. Even he, however, has remained as a property she has never in any other way been able to replace.

Catherine's partial understanding of herself becomes also a partial understanding of Morris. We wonder if he has 'made himself comfortable'. If she is right, why has he come back to her? To speak to her he says, 'would be a great satisfaction—and I have not many'. He tells Catherine, 'I have never ceased thinking of you.' Finally, he asks:

> 'Why have you never married? . . . You have had opportunities.'
> 'I didn't wish to marry.'
> 'Yes, you are rich, you are free; you have nothing to gain.'
> 'I have nothing to gain,' said Catherine.

Morris did treat Catherine abominably. His every statement above may be a calculated ploy. To see marriage in terms of 'gain' may only be cynicism. But during the scene James speaks of Morris's 'unprotected state'. Perhaps he is truthful in confessing to not having many satisfactions. As a characterization, he is not, as James acknowledged, *'fouillé'* (developed).[3] Nevertheless his life of wandering the world does suggest a rather desperate, if wayward, search for something. Like James and so many Americans of his time, he has tried Europe as a place of solace. There, however, he found no lasting focus for his life. His European wife died soon after the marriage. How *can* we think he has made himself comfortable? As dispossessed as Dr. Sloper or Catherine, he must be returning to Catherine to possess in her that steady sense of a centre to life he must have always felt he lacked. At this later, less confident, stage in his life, he will take Catherine even without her father's money. Unlike Catherine he *has* lived rather a lot. He can still face what he needs to gain.

All this is not to argue that Catherine should accept him. It is only to appreciate the structure of life from Morris's perspective. He is no more entirely a villain and a predator than is Alec d'Urberville in *Tess of the D'Urbervilles*. If Catherine understood more about Morris and what he needs from her, she might indeed have further grounds for turning him down. 'You are rich, you are free; you have nothing to gain.' How simply, from the chasm of his own despair, Morris conceives

19

Catherine's life. What a pressure she would have to lift from him. What a blankness in his life she would have to fill. Morris would want to consume her, as she had wanted to consume him. Could she answer to his demands? Yet not to answer is to be what? We do not know *how* Catherine says, 'I have nothing to gain.' She may say it with the dry irony Morris's insolence deserves. But she may also, which is awful, believe it. Such is Catherine's secure sense of containment, she now reaches out to no one and to nothing. She is content with her 'morsel of fancy-work . . . for life, as it were'.

3

'A tale purely American, the writing of which made me feel acutely the want of the "paraphernalia" '[4]—so James responded to *Washington Square*, shortly after it was written, in a letter to William Dean Howells. He was borrowing Howells's own use of the word 'paraphernalia'. Just before *Washington Square*, James had published his book on Hawthorne. In it, by way of demonstrating that 'it takes such an accumulation of history and custom, such a complexity of manners and types, to form a fund of suggestion for a novelist', he included his by now famous list of all the things American society, in contrast to European society, lacked. For James, the American novelist was unquestionably disadvantaged by the 'thinness, the blankness'[5] of the American scene.

Howells was only the first American to be offended by James's observations. In his review of *Hawthorne*, to which James's letter referred to above is a reply, Howells wrote:

> After leaving out all those novelistic 'properties' as sovereigns, courts, aristocracy, gentry, castles, cottages, cathedrals, abbeys, universities, museums, political class, Epsoms, and Ascots, by the absence of which Mr. James suggests our poverty to the English conception, we have the whole structure presenting the only fresh and novel opportunities left to fiction, opportunities manifold and inexhaustible. No man would have known less what to do with that dreary and worn-out paraphernalia than Hawthorne.[6]

More recently Richard Poirier, taking a different line from

Howells's, has observed: 'James has his reasons for insisting that Hawthorne was victimized by the social "thinness" of his environment; but . . . Hawthorne was much more the victim of literary "thickness", of "art" or "artificial system".'[7] Elsewhere, Poirier writes: 'that characters can be given a public solidity without the evocation of their place within a traditionally mannered society or even within a nationality is apparent in *Washington Square.*'[8]

Howells is obviously right to insist that American society presented fiction with fresh opportunities. But that it also gave American novelists major problems to do with point of view, characterization, and structure is an indubitable conclusion to be drawn not only from American novels themselves, but also from the pronouncements of American novelists. James's list of things absent from American society was not simply a recipe of ingredients for novels. It was an account of the structural items by reference to which European society made sense of itself. To have such paraphernalia available for a novel was also to have recourse to a way of making experience coherent. In Eliot's later terminology, one's personal talent found a place within tradition. In life and work, one participated in, or imitated, the impersonal structure of history marked out by the paraphernalia.

Poirier's observations confirm James's case rather than refute it. Hawthorne, like every major nineteenth-century American writer, is the victim of 'artificial system' because, unlike his European contemporaries, he is unsustained by any traditional system accepted as *the* view of reality. Hawthorne in *The Scarlet Letter* and James in *Washington Square* make deliberate attempts to discover a historical tradition. Chapter 3 of *Washington Square* and 'The Custom-House' prelude to the *Scarlet Letter* are explicit advertisements of the paraphernalia the respective authors have found in America. Contrary to Poirier's argument about *Washington Square*, such paraphernalia are the means by which the novel's characters are endowed with their remarkable public solidity. Indeed the paraphernalia of seventeenth-century Boston are similarly beneficial to Hawthorne. Nonetheless Washington Square, with its 'look of having had something of a social history', is perceived by James, as the order of seventeenth-century Boston is perceived by Hawthorne, to be a very recently made mark. Hawthorne's Boston is 'a new colony', 'a little town, on the edge of the western wilderness'. Washington Square has only just been built in a country where, as Arthur Townsend blithely declares, 'they invent everything all over again about every five years' (Ch. 5). In other words, for Hawthorne and James, such paraphernalia as were available could hardly be regarded as belonging to the essential system of things. The very nation itself was an artefact, recently invented on a piece of paper. Even the 'truths' which the paper declared to be 'self-evident' were self-evidently denied to large numbers of the population. How could an American writer ever be sure, in Whitman's words, 'whether that which appears so is so?'[9] How could he know anything other than 'seems'?

Such a dilemma is a challenge to the confidence of anyone seeking a firmer hold on life than Arthur Townsend's or Mrs. Penniman's. It undermines Dr. Sloper, Catherine, and Morris. Where then does it leave James? In the novel we experience his detachment from Washington Square and America, but as the novel progresses, his authorial presence becomes more and more invisible, and it is impossible to discover his attachment to anywhere else. His pleasures in the novel, unlike Dr. Sloper's, genuinely delight us. Undoubtedly his understanding of his characters' plights enacts what we would want to declare to be self-evidently a civilizing humanity. That is the bright side of the moon. The other, darker, side is that the civilizing humanity enacted may belong only to the fabrication of the novel. Outside the novel, its expectations may be as unrewarded as are Dr. Sloper's, Catherine's and Morris's. Certainly, it is only to the composition of the novel itself, and to his intercourse with us in it, that James *is* attached. Writing the novel, he puts on a mask of life.

NOTES

1. *Studies in Classic American Literature* (London, 1924), Chapter 11.
2. The numbers in parentheses refer to the chapters of *Washington Square* from which the quotations are taken.
3. F. O. Matthiessen, *The James Family* (New York, 1948), p. 325.

4. Percy Lubbock (ed.), *The Letters of Henry James* (London, 1920), I, p. 73.
5. *Hawthorne* (London, 1879), Chapter 2.
6. 'James's *Hawthorne*', *Atlantic Monthly* (February, 1880).
7. *A World Elsewhere* (London, 1968), p. 106.
8. *The Comic Sense of Henry James* (London, 1967), p. 165.
9. The words are from 'There was a child went forth.'

2

The Portrait of a Lady:
Affronting Destiny

1

The opening description of Gardencourt in *The Portrait of a Lady* suggests that James, as a man and a writer, found in Europe what he missed in America. In Europe (and especially in England where he settled) he found traditions of reality whose objectivity seemed guaranteed. Here might be relief from the necessity for American self-obsession and self-creation. The opening description of Gardencourt advertises James's acquired possession in England of the 'great deal of history' and 'complex social machinery' needed, as he saw it, 'to set a writer in motion'.[1] Gardencourt, 'built under Edward the Sixth', has for real the social history Washington Square only has the look of. It is an example of the many structural demarcations in English life. From material of this kind a reader knows what to expect, and with it a writer knows what to provide. The writer is set in motion towards the reality his reader anticipates. The solidity of presentation, such as we also get in *Emma* and *Middlemarch*, is a result.

To the end *The Portrait of a Lady* retains a kinship with the two earlier English novels. At the same time, it is radically different from either. Insofar as it is sustained by traditions of reality similar to theirs, it is sustained by what it itself reveals to be exhausted. This paradox is already apparent in the novel's very first chapter and indeed in the very first sentence.

Gardencourt enables the dramatic vividness of the opening scene on its lawn. Even so, it only sets James in motion towards the reader with what the first sentence, with deliberate bathos, describes as 'the ceremony known as afternoon tea'. The great house now provides only a diminished occasion on which an author may meet his readers. The varied, sophisticated, and ordered life, which it once epitomized, and which English novels were able to imitate and reflect, is gone. Gardencourt has passed into the hands of a 'shrewd American banker' merely as a 'great bargain'. For him, it has become no more than a huge *objet d'art*. Moreover, the banker is dying, and his sick heir, as we are to learn, is resigned to his own childless demise. The banker's visitor for afternoon tea is Lord Warburton. Formerly, his station alone would have guaranteed him. Now, he is possessed despairingly by a sense of his own hollowness and of the times' uncertainty.

In other words the traditional validities, which sustain *Emma* and *Middlemarch*, and which enable these novels to confirm realities the reader expects, are only superficially available to *The Portrait of a Lady*. According to the Preface, the novel began solely with 'the conception of a certain young woman affronting her destiny'. The choice of verb in this statement is significant. Unlike earlier English heroes and heroines, Isabel Archer does not confront. She is not facing choices, the likely results of which are established. Isabel affronts her destiny in order to provoke it to reveal itself. The possibilities of life are altogether more elusive for her than for Emma or Dorothea, or even for the Gwendolen Harleth of *Daniel Deronda*. Dr. Leavis has claimed that James, in comparison to the way George Eliot treats Gwendolen Harleth, so idealizes Isabel that 'beyond any question we are invited to share a valuation of Isabel that is incompatible with a really critical irony.'[2] In answer to this judgement, it should be understood that the problem of presenting Isabel is for James a less contained exercise than is for Jane Austen and George Eliot the problem of presenting any one of their heroines. Emma, Dorothea, and Gwendolen can be characterized so substantially, because they can be seen as part of a society of firmly established manners and opportunities. As characterizations, they belong to a confined social system and a defined

25

moral system. The moral system at least is endorsed by the author and is expected to be endorsed by the reader. We are offered no choice in *Daniel Deronda*, for example, but to decide that Gwendolen has transgressed. She travels towards the destination of moral sense and self-knowledge, where George Eliot and the reader are already awaiting her. As in most Victorian novels, the central character's journey to moral awareness serves to remind the reader what he is supposed to believe in.

James, however, does not have this firm ground to stand on when creating Isabel. He is, as the reader also may be, ahead of Isabel in experience. With Mr. Touchett he can say 'I've been through all that' (Ch. 2).[3] He has no advantage over her, however, in the absoluteness of his own knowledge. As in the last paragraph of Chapter 12, James often seems to be reading or portraying Isabel's character, even as she is reading or portraying it herself. Since 'the conception of a certain young woman affronting her destiny had begun with being all my outfit for the large building of *The Portrait of a Lady*', James's problem in composing the novel is analogous to Isabel's problem in composing herself. Consequently, we do not have the sense we have from *Emma*, *Middlemarch*, and *Daniel Deronda*, that the author is judging the action of the novel from a secure place outside it, shared with the reader. *Where* James is when not engaged in writing and reading *The Portrait of a Lady* cannot even be inferred from the novel. He engages us *within* the experience of the book, but not alongside it. He has problems, therefore, when he tries to state Isabel's character in the traditional set-piece way. In the first paragraph of Chapter 6, for example, he tells us all kinds of things about Isabel, but the information is presented rather desperately. It's as if James has a collection of ideas about her which, out of an allegiance to a traditional form of the novel, he feels anxiously obliged to place before us. The ideas remain too abstract and unfocused, however, because they are not part of anything larger than themselves. To state a character in this way, an author needs to have a character fixed in a context and to be assured of his own and the reader's position in relation to the context. These certainties are unavailable to James.

Nonetheless, he can bring 'a really critical irony' to bear on his heroine. As I shall show, his portrayal of her is not her portrayal of herself. He is aware of other areas of the canvas. He sees how she portrays other characters, who in turn portray her, and portray themselves. This act of criticism, it is true, reveals that James himself, with his characters, treads only a canvas of possible meanings, or, to take a phrase from the Preface, inhabits only a 'house of fiction'. With his characters, and with the very form of *The Portrait of a Lady*, he searches for more substantial accommodation. None is found.

2

But first Isabel as she presumptuously affronts her destiny. Take the moment at the end of Chapter 2 when, in reply to Ralph's observation that Mrs. Touchett has 'adopted' her, she replies that she is 'not a candidate for adoption', and that she is 'very fond of my liberty'. We will all be inclined to underline these pronouncements. It would be a simple reading of the novel, however, to judge Isabel literally by what she says. As Richard Poirier shrewdly observes, the opinions Isabel spouts are often 'merely trial balloons'.[4] As they occur dramatically, her proclamations are quite uncalled for by Ralph's humorous comment, and he is completely thrown by them. They are the words of a young woman who, 'with a certain visible eagerness of desire to be explicit', is as concerned to present herself to herself as to other people. What 'really critical irony' could be brought to bear on Isabel here that James doesn't bring? James knows that Isabel's is an absurdly portentous response to Ralph's casual remark, and that its emphaticalness betrays the young woman's deep uncertainty about herself, even as it demonstrates her admirable ambition. As the novel develops, he will show that Isabel will eventually ensnare herself just because, in pronouncing about liberty and other ideals, she is never wise enough to know how they might genuinely be experienced. But Isabel can only be taught by experience. Unlike Gwendolen Harleth, she is not faced by choices which with reference to authority can be defined as good and evil. As an expression of the country she comes from, she is in a position to create herself. What draws James and the reader to her is precisely the fact that, unlike her sisters and the Miss Varians (whose conventional fates we read about at the beginning of Chapters 4 and 6), she has the imagination and the bravery to want to use her freedom. Despite her own occasional 'sense of her incoherence' (Ch. 13), she will try to realize what she understands to be her best revelations about herself. For James, and eventually for Isabel herself, the most critical irony that can be brought to bear against her is that the best she is capable of should lead only to Gilbert Osmond. This outcome amounts to a crippling self-knowledge for Isabel. Nor can she ease the consciousness of how she has wasted her life by blaming, as earlier English heroes and heroines do, the worst part of herself. Hers is indeed a dark destiny which reaches forward into the twentieth century's promise of great expectations all round: one may live to the best of oneself, with the greatest opportunities, and yet arrive 'in a dark, narrow alley with a dead wall at the end' (Ch. 42).

It's with a sense of her having to be the artist of her own life that we should view Isabel's responses to both Goodwood's and Warburton's proposals of marriage. In these scenes we see how James's portrait of Isabel's portrait of herself encompasses other figures. It has not been sufficiently appreciated how the other characters in their different ways share her problem. Both Goodwood and Warburton within their contrasting public orbits are triumphant, and yet both personally are desperately unfulfilled. Their proposals are their affronting of their destinies, Warburton's case making us aware of what we also see in Hardy's work (think of Henchard, Jude and Sue), that towards the end of the nineteenth century such challenging of experience to give one an identity is no longer a uniquely American need. Both Goodwood and Warburton, by marriage to Isabel, want to provoke into reality imagined possibilities, the realization of which in any other way renders them impotent. Goodwood pursues Isabel (she is his Sue Bridehead) because in post-Civil War America she is, with her indifference to the nation's public energies in which he is embroiled, an exceptional spirit. In his portrait of their relationship she would bring beauty and spirituality into his life. She would give expression to the needs of his frustrated soul: 'he had never supposed she hadn't wings and the need of beautiful free

28

movement—he wasn't, with his own long arms and strides, afraid of any force in her' (Ch. 16). As for Warburton, who has lost that belief in himself which in an earlier generation his confrontation with his 'station' would have guaranteed, he admits half-jokingly that he needs a woman to tie 'round my neck as a life-preserver' (Ch. 1). An alliance with a 'young lady . . . from a queer country across the sea' (Ch. 12) would substantiate in his own eyes and the world's his radical posture. Indisputably (think of his sisters' reaction!), it would be a dramatic burning of his boats in which his unresolved life might be settled.

To understand the proposals in this way is to perceive how James has solicited our sympathy for Isabel's response. She refuses both suitors because she is determined not to foreclose the possibilities of her life so early by confronting destiny and becoming a wife. Moreover, in the two men's determination that she should count for so much in their lives, we can recognize something of that 'aggression' (Chs. 12, 16) she ascribes to both of them. How is she supposed to live up to the different roles they create for her? What kind of 'beautiful free movement' must she perform for Goodwood? How must she represent for Warburton, who is needled by Henrietta, that 'queer country across the sea'? To the final chapter ('I never knew *you* afraid') Goodwood is never to understand that if he is not afraid of Isabel, she is afraid of herself. To the end Warburton, who finally confronts his destiny in a marriage to 'a member of the aristocracy' (Ch. 54), never grasps that Isabel is not in Europe to give herself, but to find herself. Yet the sympathy James solicits is not only for Isabel. What distinguishes James from his fellow nineteenth-century American novelists is that he has learned from the European novel how to realize the contrasting positions of his characters in a more substantial way than by allegory and symbol. Counterbalancing Goodwood's and Warburton's portraits of Isabel are her portraits of them. She would do greater justice to the personal positions of both men if she did not persist in seeing them in metaphoric and conceptualized terms. She ought to understand that proposals are by their very nature a threat to one's freedom and that in marriage people usually do want to complete themselves by taking what they find in the other person. It's ominous that what she terms the two men's 'aggression' is also her sense of their masculinity. As the first paragraph of Chapter 17 makes clear, Isabel, in her reaction to potential sexual encounters, is excited not by the possibility of succumbing but by the triumph of rejecting. She has just seen Goodwood off, and her excitement over her 'victory' is modified not at all by her wondering earlier 'if she were not a cold, hard, priggish person' (Ch. 12).

This last quotation is only one line from Isabel's attempted portrait of herself after Warburton's proposal. It's only one example of her capacity for self-analysis and self-disapproval. No one has ever more consciously wanted to do the 'right thing' than Isabel. In this sense she contrasts with several earlier English heroes and heroines. Just as *The Portrait of a Lady* begins with characters having come from a promised land, whereas English Victorian novels usually end with characters about to step into one, so Isabel enters her novel already possessing, and possessed by, the sincere, moral ambition Victorian characters are finally left with. Unlike *Daniel Deronda*, *The Portrait of a Lady* shows that such ambition may also betray. This is why Isabel to some extent needs from Ralph advice, which is exactly the opposite of the counselling Deronda gives Gwendolen:

> Take things more easily. Don't ask youself so much whether this or that is good for you. Don't question your conscience so much—it will get out of tune like a strummed piano. Keep it for great occasions. Don't try so much to form your character—it's like trying to pull open a tight, tender young rose. Live as you like best, and your character will take care of itself. Most things are good for you; the exceptions are very rare, and a comfortable income's not one of them. . . . You've too much power of thought—above all too much conscience. . . . It's out of all reason the number of things you think wrong. (Ch. 21)

These are the words of a man who has thought a great deal about that problem of conscious living with which all the main characters of the novel are burdened. Ralph too must be the author of his own life, but he feels he is sharing the task with a partner (his illness) who will always have the final say. Deprived as he sees it of his true freedom in actuality, he affronts it in imagination. Isabel, 'living as you like best', will

30

enable him to enact 'the requirements of my imagination'
(Ch. 18). In her he can live by proxy. It is indeed he, and not
James, whom the reader identifies as strongly inclined to
idealize Isabel. She herself becomes aware of his peculiar,
parasitic involvement in her, and this knowledge is later to
make her stubbornly resistant to his advice about Osmond.
But Ralph's attitude to his cousin is not entirely self-serving. It
is also an affirmation of faith in the virtue of human nature
made by a man whose personal lot has given him little cause to
go in for such generosity of spirit. When Ralph, by para-
phrasing Iago ('I should like to put money in her purse'),
glances at the immorality of the authorial power he is assuming
over Isabel's life, we are reminded how, understandably, he
might have become poisonous. Ralph, however, always resisting the darkness, replies in the same chapter to his father's
doubts about Isabel by asserting what for many will be at least
a working creed: 'She's as good as her best opportunities' (Ch.
18). Of course he means what *he* will recognize as good and
best. At this stage he has not learned James's wisdom, that to
liberate someone is not to require them to do something of
which one will approve. Ralph is an author who wants his
character always to fulfil his hopes. He has too much at stake
on Isabel. His putting money in her purse is after all a substitute for making love to her.

Yet a great deal is lost for us all in Ralph's humiliation by
Isabel's marriage. With its roots in American idealism *The
Portrait of a Lady* has the authority to challenge our fondest
hopes. What are people if they are not as good as their best
opportunities? It's because Isabel by her marriage has been
forced to face the implications of this question for herself, that
she is wary at the end of further schemes for life. But Ralph,
even as a 'mere lattice of bones', clings to his belief in the best
possibilities. Acknowledging his culpability ('I believe I ruined
you'), still further surprised by how Isabel actually behaves
('Are you going back to him?'), he can yet say: 'I don't believe
that such a generous mistake as yours can hurt you for more
than a little' (Ch. 54). Throughout the book, Ralph's optimism
and humour are the equivalent of, and the vehicle for, the
buoyancy of tone with which James delivers to us a novel
containing so many stories of personal disappointment. Like

31

James, Ralph remains completely unembittered. Unlike George Eliot and Tom Tulliver with Maggie, James and Ralph have no investment in making Isabel 'pay' for what she has done. Life is simply worth more than this kind of morality. One pays insofar as one has the capacity for awareness. Isabel is to become aware that 'she has thrown away her life' (Ch. 42), and who can say how this self-knowledge will determine her future? Ralph is indeed very close to James despite being completely placed by the author. Watching Ralph perform in the world of *The Portrait of a Lady*, James understands how drastically more compromising it is to try to fulfil the requirements of one's imagination in life, than it is by writing a novel. What beneficial contribution to others can the authorial imagination make? James's study of Ralph's dealing with Isabel is a bleak answer for a novelist to offer to this question.

Though it's hard to believe anybody can be ready for the kind of windfall she receives, Isabel, with 'too much power of thought—above all too much conscience', was perhaps the last person to burden with a fortune. In her case, moreover, Great Expectations do not come with the promise of an established social life which she simply has to fit into. In fact her inheritance encourages her sense of superiority to the way people, whatever their ideal conception of themselves, actually find accommodation in the world. She is right to conclude that the lives of the American expatriates in Paris are 'though luxurious, inane' (Ch. 20); but in her belief that 'the world lay before her—she could do whatever she chose' (Ch. 31), she fails to understand that we are all compromising expatriates just because this kind of freedom has long been lost. Since her fortune has come to her without strings, and without her knowing by whose intervention, it confirms her too ready desire to believe in her own absoluteness. Furthermore, she is by now modelling herself on Madame Merle who at this stage in the novel always appears to Isabel's innocent, admiring eyes completely uncompromised: the very 'portrait of a lady' in the flesh as it were.

Her imitation of Madame Merle already signals a move in the direction of Osmond and is a repression in herself of those outgoing qualities which are writ large in Henrietta Stackpole. Hence her self-congratulatory approval of Madame Merle's response to Henrietta: 'Madame Merle genially squeezed her into insignificance, and Isabel felt that in foreseeing this liberality she had done justice to her friend's intelligence' (Ch. 26). It's true that Isabel and we have had earlier in the novel what the Preface recognizes as 'indubitably too much' of Henrietta, who must exasperate Isabel with her confident belief that she knows all about her friend. Henrietta knows some things, but the following words are not the lessons to teach an Isabel who has already rebuffed Goodwood and Warburton: 'You must often *dis*please others. . . . That doesn't suit you at all—you're too fond of admiration, you like to be thought well of' (Ch. 20). Even so, as one more character with reference to whom we must create our portrait of Isabel, Henrietta's career undoubtedly brings 'a really critical irony' to bear on James's heroine. Unlike Isabel she has made a life for herself amid the ways of the world. Also, in her relationship with Bantling, she concedes to her sexual nature. As Ralph puts it, 'It seems to me she's doing very well . . . going over to Paris with an ex-Lancer!' (Ch. 19). While James's affection for Henrietta is entertained by her adventures with Bantling, Isabel is amused only in order to feel superior. She is not aware that insofar as she is not to have such basic good times with a man her life will be poorer. Isabel indeed is never to be as naturally in love as even Rosier and Pansy are in love.

So when Martin Green observes disparagingly that 'the relationship between Isabel and Osmond is dangerously thin in sexual or affectionate emotion, dangerously strong in impersonal appraisal',[5] we can reply that this is a view James's portrait prompts the reader to take. We must also remember that sexual activity has everything to do with self-belief. In nineteenth-century English novels marriage, which legitimizes sexual relationships, is often the climax of the characters' discovery of their true selves. It signifies too a public confirmation of the identities discovered. The resulting, or expected, children are tokens of the characters' confidence in their ability to make an acceptable mark on the course of life.

In nineteenth-century American literature, by contrast, characters are sustained to the end by little more than their own self-questioning. They have no confidence that the self will find accommodation in the world. When first discovered by her aunt, Isabel is secluded in 'a mysterious apartment which lay beyond the library' (Ch. 3). Perhaps, in Emily Dickinson's unflinching but resilient words, she is thinking 'It might be lonelier without the loneliness.' So habitual, so intense, so cerebral, has been Isabel's self-scrutinizing, she has almost unsexed herself. Like Sue Bridehead, who is the product of unaccommodating times in late nineteenth-century England, she hardly has left in her the conventional sexual appetite which survives in Henrietta. Consequently, when she affronts sexual experience (and the transition from solipsist to wilful affronter is entirely logical), she has only a theoretical sense of a relationship with a man: 'to prefer Gilbert Osmond as she preferred him was perforce to break all other ties. She tasted of the sweets of this preference, and they made her conscious, almost with awe, of the invidious and remorseless tide of the charmed and possessed condition, great as was the traditional honour and imputed virtue of being in love' (Ch. 35). How wonderfully James captures here Isabel's ardent, theoretical nature. She accepts Osmond not only because he alone seems to have established a life of personal, uncompromised value, but also because, in contrast to Goodwood's and Warburton's complicating pressures, he initially makes no demands even when he proposes: 'You may heed it now or never as you please' (Ch. 29). For his part, his despairing, desolate soul ('I'm sick of my adorable taste' (Ch. 22)) is briefly uplifted by the opportunity to ally himself to, and to capture, an unblemished idealism he can still envy. Very soon after the marriage, however, because by its very nature such idealism condemns what his life amounts to, Isabel becomes contemptible to him.

3

It's from Chapter 42, when Isabel sits through the night meditating on her relationship with her husband, that we learn nearly everything about the marriage. For James, writing the Preface more than twenty years after the novel's publication, this chapter was 'obviously the best thing in the book'. 'Reduced to its essence,' he observes, 'it is but the vigil of searching criticism; but it throws the action further forward than twenty "incidents" might have done.' There can be few readers willing to accept these judgements without demur. For a start, Chapter 42 has to perform functions unmentioned by James. It has to throw the action *backwards* to the early years of the marriage, restore to the reader his close relationship with Isabel, and thereby rescue the reader from the sense of dislocation he has felt since the end of Chapter 35 when he left Isabel on the verge of marriage. All readers, as they began Chapter 36, will have been more prepared for some direct treatment of Isabel's early married life than they are for what they get: a defiantly announced date revealing that three years have passed, and a re-introduction to Mr. Edward Rosier whom, in James's unblushing words, 'the reader will perhaps not have forgotten!' Why is it that James has not given us directly the first three years of the marriage? We undoubtedly miss what is not presented. We may decide that James was incapable of writing the required scenes. Indeed I think this is the case, and yet I want to argue that the incapacity is not simply a lack of talent for creating objectively a certain kind of experience. James does not present Isabel's and Osmond's first three years of marriage, because he never believed in the marriage as a possible sustenance for Isabel. He always knows her affronting will be unaccommodated by the world. Consequently, when Isabel believes her destiny has revealed itself to be marriage to Osmond, James can give the enactment of her hopes and the process of disillusion nothing more than a distanced treatment. He only resumes his former intimacy with her when, in Chapter 42, he can present her reflection on a failure which for him was always inevitable.

There is indeed a close parallel between Isabel's career and the form of *The Portrait of a Lady*. As Isabel finds no self-fulfilment in the social institution of marriage, so *The Portrait of a Lady* itself is finally unsustained by Europe's 'great deal of history' and 'complex social machinery'. After the marriage, *The Portrait of a Lady* loses its forward momentum. It no longer even affects to believe in possible choices to be made in an observed public world. With its heroine, it turns essentially inward.

What follows continues nonetheless to be James's portrait of

Isabel's portrait of herself. Our relationship to her remains dynamic. Isabel has much to learn, and not only factually. After her marriage, she more than ever desires to imitate Madame Merle and to make, as she is convinced the older lady does, 'her will [the] mistress of her life' (Ch. 40). But she has yet to appreciate out of what shameful sense of failure, and consequently with what 'courage' Madame Merle wears her mask of life. She understands these things when the two 'ladies' meet for the last time in Chapter 52. The encounter is one of those moments a novel of *The Portrait of a Lady*'s developed length can give us. It depends so much on the reader's memory of Isabel's and Madame Merle's early exchanges, for example in Chapter 19. Then Isabel was all innocent admiration for what she conceived simply as her new acquaintance's 'talents, accomplishments, aptitudes'. Madame Merle, for her part, was then agreeably refreshed and entertained by the virgin ambition of a young woman she was able to handle with one stained hand behind her back. In Chapter 52 Isabel understands out of what abyss of disappointment and unfulfilment Madame Merle's manner has matured. Now she comprehends that if she is to portray herself to the world as a lady, it may be only to conceal a similar emptiness in her own life.

It's Isabel's self-recognition in Madame Merle at this moment, her seeing 'it all as distinctly as if it had been reflected in a large clear glass', that de-fuses the outspoken revenge she is very tempted to take on the older lady. Or rather, the self-recognition confines the revenge to silence, to leaving Madame Merle, 'the cleverest woman in the world', in the 'unprecedented situation' of 'knowing as little what to think as the meanest'. Again James asks us to contemplate all the angles of *his* portrayal of the scene. Undoubtedly, Isabel's conduct towards Madame Merle, prompted by the failure she recognizes they have both made of their lives, is charitable on both their behalfs. Later in the chapter, she can even tell Pansy: 'You must never say . . . that you don't like Madame Merle.' Yet Isabel's silence does leave Madame Merle in a position of 'helplessness', and we are told by James that Isabel would never 'accuse' Madame Merle because 'she would never give [Madame Merle] the opportunity to defend herself.'

Isabel's continuing pride, which has always defensively cut her off from the advice and sympathy of others, cannot let Madame Merle have her moment. Indeed, insofar as Isabel sees all of this meeting 'as if it had been reflected in a large clear glass', she doesn't see Madame Merle. She doesn't appreciate how readily her former friend, who has been a *lover*, would give herself to some act of mutual consolation. Because Isabel cannot respond to the older lady's needs, Madame Merle, when Isabel returns from seeing Pansy, finds herself striving to restore their relationship to its earlier status. To regain the superiority over Isabel she always enjoyed, she vainly tells Isabel it was Ralph who was responsible for her money. Sadly, her final triumph over Isabel does nothing to relieve her profound unhappiness over her life's betrayal of her own and Isabel's best hopes.

To the end, James does bring 'a really critical irony' to bear on Isabel. He is always aware of the life she is separated from by her withdrawal into her consciousness. Her affronting becomes too aesthetic an enterprise. Reflecting on her marriage, she thinks: 'the finest—in the sense of being the subtlest—manly organism she had ever known had become her property, and the recognition of her having but to put out her hands and take it had been originally a sort of act of devotion' (Ch. 42). The words reveal Isabel to have collected Osmond as a sort of *objet d'art*. She knows now that he is not the property she invested in, but she does not understand that to see a man in this way is not to take him as a husband. Had Osmond even been what she imagined, marriage to him on these terms would have been a queer affair. Surely, she must some day come to terms with the masculinity she feels to be 'justified' by the kiss Goodwood gives her in their extraordinary last encounter.

The final scene with Goodwood points towards Lawrence's dramatization of sexual experience as a possible discovery of absolute self. It is territory closed to Isabel and (one must say too) to James, though often he brings his characters to the very edge of it and implies their need to venture into it. James, like Lawrence, wants to believe in some possibility of absolute definition. Without it, against what is one to measure one's life? What sense of self can one affirm and live by? As *The*

Portrait of a Lady comes to an end, Isabel can have no confidence that her future will necessarily be brighter than her past. What she has learned guarantees her nothing. The self which judges the self, knowing where its best aspirations have led, remains the very self that promoted delusion. With this knowledge, Isabel's thoughts about her future life, for example at the end of the second paragraph of Chapter 53, can only be indeterminate: 'the middle years wrapped about her again and the grey curtain of indifference closed her in.'

James, for his part, if he ever were in a position equivalent to Isabel's, would always have another book to write. He transcends her fate by writing about it. For him, too, affronting was an aesthetic enterprise. He acknowledges as much in a famous letter of September 1867 to T. S. Perry: 'to be an American is an excellent preparation for culture. . . . We can deal freely with forms of civilization not our own, can pick and choose and assimilate and in short (aesthetically and etc) claim our property where we find it. . . . We must of course have something of our own . . . and I take it that we shall find it in our moral consciousness, our unprecedented spiritual lightness and vigour.' What a momentous fate James announces here! Given such opportunities, what could the Americans James describes ever settle for? They would always be ardent for completeness, while the inevitable sense of incompleteness resulting from a life so deliberately pursued would have nothing traditional to fall back onto. By the time of *The Portrait of a Lady*, moreover, James was no longer so sure about 'our moral consciousness'. To turn to that faculty is to begin a journey through crooked corridors, which are unwinding themselves in Chapter 42, and which are the veritable empire of the Governess in *The Turn of the Screw*. In other words, the boundary lines between moral consciousness, fantasy, and neurosis, are slipping. Isabel and the Governess are antecedents of Joseph K. To be an American is to be a modern, exiled from traditional sureties, affronting uncertainty.

With respect to Isabel, therefore, James's irony must finally be very much the irony of identification with her. Her affronting has provided her with more grounds for self-scrutiny than she could ever have longed for. As we leave her, we can only wish for her the resilience and buoyancy of her creator. For him, *The Portrait of a Lady* contains self-reflections Isabel has even yet to encounter.

NOTES

1. *Hawthorne* (London, 1879), Chapter 1.
2. *The Great Tradition* (London, 1948), Chapter 2.
3. All quotations from *The Portrait of a Lady* are taken from the New York Edition, 1908. The numbers in parentheses refer to chapters from this edition.
4. *The Comic Sense of Henry James* (London, 1960), p. 215.
5. *Re-appraisals* (London, 1963), p. 157.

3

The Bostonians:
Experience and
Adventures

1

I take the title to this chapter from *The Ambassadors*. In that
novel we are invited by James to be indulgently aware that
Lambert Strether, the central character, is a man capable
of 'an amount of experience out of any proportion to his
adventures'.[1] What James means by 'experience' in this context is the inward life of Strether's consciousness. By 'adventures' he means involvement in an outward, worldly life.
Using this distinction, we recognize Strether as one more in a
long line of Jamesian characters portrayed predominantly in
terms of the experience of their consciousness. A possible consequence of this predominance is that James's novels may
themselves be accused of indulging their characters' experience out of any proportion to adventures. For some readers
indeed this will be a fundamental charge against which his
novels have hardly any defence. For others, the defence con-
sists not only in the significance of the experience presented by
the novels, but also in the recognition they give to adventures
the central characters *don't* have. Their endorsement of the
adventures of a Henrietta Stackpole or a Jim Pocock, for
example, contributes to their critical exhibition of the experience of an Isabel Archer or Lambert Strether. Nonetheless,

40

even lovers of James must admit that such adventures take place, when they are presented at all, at the edges of his novels. Moreover they are often not directly realized, with the result that criticism of a central character is at best covertly implied or putative. In the case of Merton Densher of *The Wings of a Dove*, we find ourselves thinking of adventures he is not having as a young man and perhaps should be having. Surely, he spends some time doing something with male friends, colleagues, associates, or acquaintances. Nowhere in the novel as a whole, however, do we find an adequate expression of such alternatives to his experience.

I choose to raise the subject of experience and adventures at the outset of a chapter on *The Bostonians*, precisely because *The Bostonians* is the one novel by James which most obviously turns its attention to life in an outward and worldly sense. *The Bostonians* has no centre of consciousness. In it, James makes his points in a very direct authorial voice. As Irving Howe has shown in his indispensable study of the novel,[2] it deals with the entanglement of personal and public issues in Boston and New York in the period immediately following the Civil War. Yet it might be claimed that even *The Bostonians* confirms the limitations of James's ability to present adventures in the sense defined above. Certainly, James himself was aware of the novel's faults. He confessed to his brother:

> All the middle part is too diffuse and insistent—far too describing and explaining and expatiating. The whole thing is too long and dawdling. This came from the fact (partly) that I had the sense of knowing terribly little about the kind of life I had attempted to describe.[3]

'All the middle part' of *The Bostonians* is the pages which should develop the lives of the three main characters (Olive Chancellor, Verena Tarrant, and Basil Ransom) beyond the triangle in which the early chapters of the novel place them. In these pages they should have adventures. What, we wonder, are Olive and Verena reading, and whom are they meeting, as they prepare themselves for their decisive campaigns? When we are told in Chapter 20 that they frequent the best musical occasions in Boston, why does not James actually give us the adventure of a concert? Such a scene would not be out of place in a novel which needs to present something of Boston life in the 1870s. Nor would it be out of place for James to allow more prominence than he does to the supposedly ambitious life and work of Basil Ransom in New York.

James seemingly cannot move, when he needs to develop these three characters beyond the initial positions in which he has conceived them. This is why *The Bostonians* has hardly anywhere to go with Olive, Verena and Basil after the first twelve chapters. By this stage we have had in its entirety Olive's and Basil's rivalry for possession of Verena. There is to be no development of the issues involved in this rivalry. Consequently, since Olive and Ransom are very much the issues they voice, there is to be little development of their characters. In an essentially personal drama, which considering the themes the novel purports to treat has insufficient public dimension, Verena exchanges her commitment to the bigoted Olive for commitment to the bigoted Basil. Why she must choose Basil from all the other men she might have met is hard to say. His relationship with her involves very little of the adventures of a lover and his lass.

'This came from the fact (partly) that I had the sense of knowing terribly little about the kind of life I had attempted to describe.' Omit 'partly' from James's statement, and we have as much explanation as we need to account for what is missed in *The Bostonians*. Omit 'partly' indeed, and we also have an explanation in James's letter for all the other adventures his fiction is without. Why are his characters on the whole so stripped of resources? Why are they so deprived of the unscheming and untreacherous relations and friends, the instinctive pleasures, the jobs, the habits, the talents, the achievements, the good meals, that keep most of us going? Is it because James, so dedicated to the *art* of fiction, so inveterately a spectator at life's feast, knew terribly little about the adventures such things provide? Is this why most of his central characters are so exclusively (for many readers too exclusively) thrust in on their intensely private experience?

'Partly' will always be one answer to these last two rhetorical questions. Yet the issues they raise must be taken further. We need to ask ourselves how integral to the nature of life are the resources listed above. Would they be present under any conditions? Or are they (even instinctive pleasures) dependent on a considerable degree of stability and precedent? In the major nineteenth-century American novels whose very material is the unprecedented, the central characters are generally deprived of the above resources. Nor is it an accident that in *Jude the Obscure*, when at the end of the nineteenth century in England the certainties of Victorian civilization and its abundantly adventurous novels are gone, we find characters as unaccommodated by the world, and as desperately uncertain of even sexual identity, as any in American fiction. Times are strained in Hardy's novel. Whatever Jude and Sue seek is unforthcoming. There are no eternal resources they can simply revert to.

Times are strained in *The Bostonians* too, notwithstanding the apparent confidence of its tone and the surety with which it 'states' its characters. The novel is set in the immediate aftermath of the Civil War. If after Chapter 12 it has hardly anywhere to go with its three main characters, where could we expect it to go? Where does a nation go (especially the American nation in 1870) after a civil war? This question takes its force from the fact that in the nineteenth-century American imagination the only destination to be settled for (by the nation, or by a novel, poem, or play) was always the ideal. In the long-fallen, old world, disillusion and compromise were institutionalized in structures that literature could realistically imitate. America, by contrast, was gifted with the requirements to meet its imagination of the best. That the best was not reached deprived American writers of belief in the virtue of any destination. What had America, with its resources for life, liberty and the pursuit of happiness, to do with slavery and civil war? What grounds, what purposes did these catastrophes provide for further adventures?

These last two questions are at the heart of the darkness in *Adventures of Huckleberry Finn*, a book in which the adventures make no sense at all. *Huckleberry Finn* is set in pre-Civil War times, but it is a post-Civil War book. It was published within a year of *The Bostonians*. Extracts from it appeared in *Century* during the period *The Bostonians* was being serialized in that magazine.[4] It casts a great deal of light on James's novel. In *Huckleberry Finn*, Twain has the experience, Huck the adventures. The experience of the South, never since more vividly realized, cannot be coherently accommodated in any structure of adventures. Only humour, more and more for its own sake, keeps the author going to an end wilfully ridiculous and contrived. After a civil war in America, and if one were not to settle for what Twain labelled 'the Gilded Age', where was there to go with a novel or with life?

The question is implicit in the formal dead-end which *The Bostonians* represents for James. In its opening three chapters and elsewhere, there is every sign that James was attempting to write in *The Bostonians* what Dr. Leavis thought he had written. In line with some of James's own recent pronouncements in 'The Art of Fiction' (1884), *The Bostonians* would be a novel as full of 'solidity of specification' concerning characters and their environment as any novel in the great nineteenth-century English tradition. All would be enlivened by intelligent, entertaining authorial comment, frequently displaying itself in this case in a satirical energy which owed much to, and at its best even rivalled, Dickens's. We would be in the hands of a writer who, in Dr. Leavis's words, 'brings to the business of the novelist a wide intellectual culture, as well as, in an exceptionally high degree, the kind of knowledge of individual humans and concrete societies that we expect of a great novelist'.[5]

But notice how Leavis's words ('brings to the business') suggest a writer who already has his values and his position established *outside* of the novel and before he begins it. This stance was one Jane Austen, George Eliot and Dickens could take with genuine confidence. It enabled them to relate to the reader alongside the fiction through commonly shared beliefs and assumptions. It helped to define their novels' solidity of specification and the range of adventures available to their characters. For James as an American, however, such a stance could only be an affectation. He takes it in *The Bostonians*, but as in *Washington Square* and *The Portrait of a Lady*, it is subverted from within the novel itself. No one in *The Bostonians*, and probably no one in post-Civil War America, is genuinely sustained by the established hierarchies of culture and class the stance depends on. Olive Chancellor, who might have been expected to be an upholder of the hierarchies, wants to turn her back on them. Basil Ransom has seen his particular heritage of them destroyed. Insofar as they had played a part in the civilizing of America, they did not indeed prevent a civil war. Now they survive only to be exploited by the likes of Mrs. Luna and Mrs. Burrage, or to be aspired to by the 'demoralized' (Ch. 10)[6] Mrs. Tarrant.

In other words the very values which guarantee mid-nineteenth century English realism and Leavis's 'Great Tradition' turn out to be of doubtful relevance to James's material in *The Bostonians*. I am not saying James explicitly recognizes his deprivation in the novel itself. In fact, it's apparent in *The Bostonians* that James is confident he can offer in the novel the realism he missed in Hawthorne generally and the satire he particularly missed in *The Blithedale Romance*. He regretted that the reformers in *The Blithedale Romance* 'came off so easily'.[7] In reaching this conclusion, however, he betrayed the simplicity of his response to Hawthorne's novel. He did not understand that satire may be absent from Hawthorne's novel, because Hawthorne did not presume to know on behalf of what satire should be written. When the bonds of a recently invented country are as indistinguishable from their counterfeits as they are in *The Blithedale Romance*, *The Confidence Man*, *Adventures of Huckleberry Finn* and *The Bostonians* itself, how can any artist be sure his own invention is the real thing? Miles Coverdale, the narrator of *The Blithedale Romance* and undoubtedly a surrogate for Hawthorne, is incapacitated by self-doubt of this kind. He knows that the actuality he tries to recover after twelve years is inseparable from the story he is telling himself about it. He is the kind of 'centre' and reflector of his creator's problems such as James himself uses in many works other than *The Bostonians*.

In *The Bostonians* James is more presumptuous. He obviously felt the frauds let loose after the Civil War were fair game for his satire. *The Bostonians* makes us laugh a lot. It has plenty of that 'American humour' which in *Hawthorne* James claimed was the American writer's 'consolation' in his 'terrible denudation'.[8] How much James's humour consoles him in *The Bostonians* is for any individual reader to judge. To me, James as he writes the novel is as unrelieved of experience as are Olive and Basil within the novel. Like Hawthorne's, Melville's and Twain's, his humour fills the gap between the ideal and the fall. It gets the author by, and we are grateful for where we have been with him. It leaves him, however, where the other three are left—nowhere.

2

Yet the novel begins confidently enough. With phrases from *Hawthorne* in our ears, we recognize in the first three chapters that post-Civil War America undoubtedly has enough history and social machinery to set a writer solidly in motion. In the 1870s, it affords a novelist the paraphernalia and typologies out of which the characters in the opening three chapters are created. Basil Ransom is a conservative from the defeated and provincial South, hungry physically and intellectually, but maybe pretending to more stature than he really has. Mrs. Luna is a widow from New York, experienced in Europe and on the lookout for sexual adventures. Olive Chancellor, her sister, has inherited among other things over two hundred years of Boston self-torture on behalf of public morality. It is in relation to Boston culture that the South is seen as provincial, even though Boston culture is now in a state of enervation with 'books . . . on little shelves like brackets (as if a book were a statuette)' (Ch. 3). Similarly, it is in relation to Boston rigour that New York and Europe are seen as lax, though Boston rigour, as embodied in Olive, now finds itself searching for causes: 'it was in her nature to look for duties, to appeal to her conscience for tasks' (Ch. 2).

During the opening scenes in Olive's parlour, James maintains an easy balance of perspective. He presents the characters from his own point of view, or adopts one of theirs, allowing what they see in one another to be also a definition of themselves. Altogether, if we come with Dr. Leavis from Jane Austen and George Eliot, we are on familar ground in these and several other scenes in the novel, such as Olive's interview with Mrs. Burrage in Chapter 32. The scenes take their substance from a firmly established context of manners (Boston and New York bourgeois) deriving ultimately from English conventions. Mrs. Burrage's type of powerful matriarch, for example, will appear again as the English Mrs. Lowder (a frustrated matriarch) in *The Wings of a Dove*. With this sort of material, James knows where he is and expects his audience to know where *it* is. It should know how people are expected to behave in the given situations. Hence the humour when the conventions are by-passed, as in this visit by Matthias Pardon to Olive:

> She thought Mr Pardon's visit a liberty; but if she expected to convey this idea to him by witholding any suggestion that he should sit down, she was greatly mistaken, inasmuch as he cut the ground from under her feet by himself offering her a chair. His manner represented hospitality enough for both of them. (Ch. 17)

At the beginning of Chapter 4, however, we have left Olive's parlour, and we meet this account of Miss Birdseye:

> She was a little old lady, with an enormous head; that was the first thing Ransom noticed—the vast, fair, protuberant, candid, ungarnished brow, surmounting a pair of weak, kind, tired-looking eyes, and ineffectually balanced in the rear by a cap which had the air of falling backward, and which Miss Birdseye suddenly felt for while she talked, with unsuccessful irrelevant movements. She had a sad, soft, pale face, which (and it was the effect of her whole head) looked as if it had been soaked, blurred, and made vague by exposure to some slow dissolvent. The long practice of philanthropy had not given accent to her features; it had rubbed out their transitions, their meanings. The waves of sympathy, of enthusiasm, had wrought upon them in the same way in which the waves of time finally modify the surface of old marble busts, gradually washing away their sharpness, their details. . . .
>
> She always dressed in the same way: she wore a loose black jacket, with deep pockets, which were stuffed with papers, memoranda of a voluminous correspondence; and from beneath her jacket depended a short stuff dress. The brevity of this simple garment was the one device by which Miss Birdseye managed to suggest that she was a woman of business, that she wished to be free for action. She belonged to the Short-Skirts League, as a matter of course; for she belonged to any and every league that had been founded for almost any purpose whatever. This did not prevent her being a confused, entangled, inconsequent, discursive old woman, whose charity began at home and ended nowhere, whose credulity kept pace with it, and who knew less about her fellow-creatures, if possible, after fifty years

47

of humanitary zeal, than on the day that she had gone into the field to testify against the inequity of most arrangements. Basil Ransom knew very little about such a life as hers, but she seemed to him a relevation of a class, and a multitude of socialistic figures, of names and episodes that he had heard of, grouped themselves behind her. She looked as if she had spent her life on platforms, in audiences, in conventions, in phalansteries, in *seances*; in her faded face there was a kind of reflection of ugly lecture-lamps; with its habit of an upward angle, it seemed turned toward a public speaker, with an effort of respiration in the thick air in which social reforms are usually discussed. She talked continually, in a voice of which the spring seemed broken, like that of an overworked bell-wire; and when Miss Chancellor explained that she had brought Mr Ransom because he was so anxious to meet Mrs Farrinder, she gave the young man a delicate, dirty, democratic little hand, looking at him kindly, as she could not help doing, but without the smallest discrimination as against others who might not have the good furtune (which involved, possibly, an injustice), to be present on such an interesting occasion. She struck him as very poor, but it was only afterward that he learned she had never had a penny in her life. No one had an idea how she lived; whenever money was given her she gave it away to a negro or a refugee. No woman could be less invidious, but on the whole she preferred these two classes of the human race. Since the Civil War much of her occupation was gone, for before that her best hours had been spent in fancying that she was helping some Southern slave to escape. It would have been a nice question whether, in her heart of hearts, for the sake of this excitement, she did not sometimes wish the blacks back in bondage.

Most readers will find this an excessively final statement for a novelist to make so early about a character whom we have not yet been allowed to see for herself. Suddenly we have lost the balance and proportion of the first three chapters. James's prose here becomes so self-generating that it's impossible to imagine a Miss Birdseye who embodies all the attributes he describes. We may actually see as a result of the passage a little old lady dressed in a certain way. When we reach the description of the 'effect' of Miss Birdseye's 'whole head', however, we already feel we are responding more to the inordinacy of James's desire to ridicule the 'long practice of philanthropy' than to an actualized character. Could someone as evidently restless as Miss Birdseye (think of her voluminous correspondence and continuous talk) ever be appropriately compared to an old marble bust? As we read further, do we believe that anyone really would belong 'to any and every league that had been founded for any purpose whatever'? If someone were so chaotically committed, would it not entail their being 'confused', rather than as James puzzlingly says 'prevent' it? How would Miss Birdseye have to look, to look as if she had 'spent her life' as James goes on to say? Can we imagine a 'little old lady' looking thus? Can we imagine seeing in her 'faded face' a 'kind of reflection of ugly lecture lamps'? Why are the lecture lamps ugly? Why is 'social reform' usually discussed in 'thick air'? Why is a quality ascribed to Miss Birdseye's voice which it never actually has when she speaks? What kind of relationship do 'dirty' and 'democratic' have?

In this castigation of Miss Birdseye we get authorial ideology extravagantly at the expense of characterization. This is why the use of Basil's point of view in the above passage is not, as it was in response to Olive in the first three chapters, dynamic. When Basil looked at Olive, we were aware there was more to Olive than he saw. In Miss Birdseye's case, by contrast, he sees the truth. His point of view is only a substitute for James's. After beginning with Basil's point of view, therefore, James can immediately ignore it. Later, when he briefly returns to it, he presents it uncritically, even though he confesses remarkably that 'Basil Ransom knew very little about such a life as hers.'

There is indeed a connection between James's animus in response to Miss Birdseye and his urbanity in presenting the first three chapters. The ideology James implicitly upholds in his condemnation of Miss Birdseye is the very hierarchy of conventions and values which enable him to dramatize Chapters 1 to 3, and which will provide for many other episodes in the novel. James is anxious to nail Miss Birdseye, because for him she represents attitudes which will cut from under his feet the very ground for the writing we find in the first three chapters. Miss Birdseye (an 'essentially formless old woman, who had no more outline than a bundle of hay', her features without 'transitions' and 'meanings', her greetings 'without the smallest discrimination', her life utterly democratic and public), deprives a novelist relying on the hierarchies of complex social machinery of his hold on life. She even deprives novels of any place in the world, since the reading of novels depends on a minimum of 'organized privacy . . . habits and tastes' (Ch. 3).

'Organized privacy . . . habits and tastes' are what Basil Ransom feels himself in the presence of in Olive's house. His response to a Boston parlour is admittedly that of a provincial. In this respect it anticipates that of Lambert Strether in *The Ambassadors* (also a provincial, but now from Massachusetts itself) to dwellings in Paris. Such a connection between Basil and Strether reminds us that values are indeed relative. Nonetheless, even James has to set some store in *The Bostonians* on what Boston culture and conventions stand for. Without giving them some endorsement, how can he 'do' Matthias Pardon when the young man visits Olive in her own house and himself offers her a chair? If it were not an accepted convention that a visitor should wait to be asked to sit down, James would have no point to make about Matthias Pardon at this moment. He would have no meaning to give the character and probably wouldn't even have a character, since Matthias Pardon is done throughout the novel in terms of the conventions he violates.

The confrontation between Olive and Matthias Pardon has therefore a deeper meaning than similar oppositions would have in Jane Austen and George Eliot. James recognizes the young man's audacity to be dismissive not only of the manner in which Olive seeks security on this occasion, but also (like Miss Birdseye's formlessness) of the manner in which he is claiming security as he writes the novel. In fact all the characters who make up the 'world' of the novel (Miss Birdseye, Mrs. Farrinder, The Tarrants, Matthias Pardon) are a similar threat to James. This is why James's stating of these characters is out of all proportion to any dramatic adventures they are allowed. James's statings of the characters conceals his insecurity with them. It ensures they confirm his experience and thus gives him a kind of mastery over them. Of Mrs. Tarrant, for example, we read:

Public speaking had been a Greenstreet tradition, and if Mrs Tarrant had been asked whether in her younger years she had ever supposed she would marry a mesmeric healer, she would have replied: 'Well, I never thought I should marry a gentleman who would be silent on the platform!' This was her most general humiliation; it included and exceeded every other, and it was a poor consolation that Selah possessed as a substitute— his career as a healer, to speak of none other, was there to prove it—the eloquence of the hand. The Greenstreets had never set much store on manual activity; they believed in the influence of the lips. (Ch. 10)

There are probably very few readers who have not laughed at this passage. I have laughed at it myself many times. The way 'eloquence of the hand' becomes 'manual activity' hints wonderfully at Selah Tarrant's relationship with his predominantly female clients. In turn 'manual activity' leads to the supposedly contrasting 'influence of the lips' but, with the intimacy of 'lips', makes us wonder whether the 'Greenstreet tradition' was itself very different from Selah's exploits.

Yet, to think further about the passage is to become aware, as with the account of Miss Birdseye, that it only allows character to exist on its own contrived terms. We are never actually to see in the novel a Mrs. Tarrant who enacts the condition James ascribes to her. Nor do we believe that her reply to the question about her marriage would have been as measured as the statement James puts in her mouth. In any case, and putting it bluntly, who cares? In post-Civil War America especially, if it is as *The Bostonians* represents it to be, who will want to be led such a journey over all James's self-underlining definite articles? The urbanity of his prose and the reading habits it relies on are strikingly at odds with the material and the age it is coming to terms with. This incongruity contributes to the humour of course, but it also reveals James's prose to be one more American structure without foundation in what it is imposed on. In Wallace Stevens's terms it is another jar in Tennessee.

After *The Bostonians* and *The Princess Casamassima* (both published in the same year), James was never again to reveal his hand in a novel in so many direct statements. In a letter to his brother in which he defended himself against the accusation that Miss Birdseye was based on Elizabeth Peabody, Hawthorne's sister-in-law, he declared that the character 'was evolved entirely from my moral consciousness, like every other person I have ever drawn'.[9] Whether this affirmation is true or not, it becomes a useful reminder of how his novels after *The Bostonians* and *The Princess Casamassima* (and indeed how much of *The Portrait of a Lady*) work. Isabel and Strether, for example, evolve other characters from their moral consciousness. Like James in *The Bostonians*, they too want to convert character-type into the absolute truth about an individual. The point about *The Portrait of a Lady* and *The Ambassadors*, however, is that Isabel's and Strether's recourse to moral consciousness is part of James's critical exhibition of their lives. In *The Bostonians*, by contrast, he himself takes Isabel's and Strether's short cut to meaning. He does not want to imagine that Miss Birdseye's adventures may have a significance other than that determined by his own moral experience and vision of America.

He is led to presume too much on his own objectivity, because *The Bostonians* lacks the kind of 'centre' that Isabel becomes in *The Portrait of a Lady* and that Maisie and Strether are throughout their respective novels. James clearly felt he could be as 'objective to his own vision'[10] in this novel, as he had diagnosed Daudet to be in *Evangeliste*, a novel he used as a model for *The Bostonians*. In any case, he did not have in *The Bostonians* the kind of character which appealed to him as a centre. James is drawn to exhibit from the inside Isabel, Maisie, Fleda Vetch, Strether, Merton Densher and Maggie Verver, because they all live very much in terms of their moral and aesthetic experience. As they compose their lives in their books, they are surrogates for James's composition of his own life which includes their books.

For neither Olive nor Basil, the two main forces in *The Bostonians*, can James feel such an affinity. Olive wants to live, in Irving Howe's term, by her 'desires'. In exposing herself to violations of her taste, she is revealed to be making the kind of instinctive criticism of taste that James makes of the characters he uses as centres. James does not support her rebellion, however, because it unnerves him. He knows that the taste of 'the *bourgeoisie*—the oldest and best' in Boston does not amount to very much. Without even it, nonetheless, what is left in the

America of the 1870s? Will the end of things be anything more than the unregulated exploitation and freakishness such as is found at large in *The Bostonians*? At the personal level, will Olive's adventures amount to anything more than confusion, masochism and self-perversion?

Not that James is without sympathy for Olive. He mocks her aims, but pities deeply her plight. No one knows more about estrangement than the exiled James. Like Olive, he himself has wandered alone through city streets out of a determined need to 'mingle in the common life' (Ch. 3). His exile in Europe, however, gave him a perspective on the self and on America. Life in an older civilization can relieve one of the burden of carrying one's life in one's own, inevitably inadequate hands. For Olive, estranged in America, there is no such relief. Her passions confusing her ideology, her ideology frustrating her passions, she falls through the thin surface of American order. The consequence (almost the necessary consequence) for her, as for some later American radicals, is personal chaos.

Basil Ransom may seem the very opposite of Olive. Even so, we should not feel he takes things as easily as he claims. A man who has seen the expected structure of his life cataclysmically wrecked, he clings to traditional notions of male and female roles as to a last floating plank of reassurance. *His* estrangement (equal to Olive's) is evident in the concluding lines of this account of where he lives in New York:

> Basil Ransom lived in New York, rather far to the eastward, and in the upper reaches of the town; he occupied two small shabby rooms in a somewhat decayed mansion which stood next to the corner of the Second Avenue. The corner itself was formed by a considerable grocer's shop, the near neighbourhood of which was fatal to any pretensions Ransom and his fellow-lodgers might have had in regard to gentility of situation. . . . The two sides of the shop were protected by an immense penthouse shed, which projected over a greasy pavement and was supported by wooden posts fixed in the curbstone. Beneath it, on the dislocated flags, barrels and baskets were freely and picturesquely grouped; an open cellarway yawned beneath the feet of those who might pause to gaze too fondly on the savoury wares displayed in the window; a strong odour of smoked fish,

combined with a fragrance of molasses, hung about the spot; the pavement, towards the gutters, was fringed with dirty panniers, heaped with potatoes, carrots, and onions; and a smart, bright waggon, with the horse detached from the shafts, drawn up on the edge of the abominable road (it contained holes and ruts a foot deep, and immemorial accumulations of stagnant mud), imparted an idle, rural, pastoral air to a scene otherwise perhaps expressive of a rank civilisation. The establishment was of the kind known to New Yorkers as a Dutch grocery; and red-faced, yellow-haired, bare-armed vendors might have been observed to lounge in the door-way. I mention it not on account of any particular influence it may have had on the life or thoughts of Basil Ransom, but for old acquaintance sake and that of local colour; besides which, a figure is nothing without a setting, and our young man came and went every day, with rather an indifferent, unperceiving step, it is true, among the objects I have briefly designated. (Ch. 21)

Basil's 'indifferent and unperceiving step' betrays a pitiful doggedness of purpose. It's as if he must contain and protect such individual sense of self as he has left. He can risk no distractions. His uncertainty, paradoxically, is why he is so assertive on behalf of 'the masculine character' (Ch. 34). In this cause he finds a definition of himself such as he has not had since his participation in the Civil War. Since the cause is, however, as much a cover-up of personal emptiness as is Selah Tarrant's 'eternal waterproof' (Ch. 13), it can never assure him of himself. Basil never has enough confidence of self even to acknowledge his need of Verena. He is not the lover to Verena's lass because, as the end of Chapter 37 humorously reveals ('Verena listened to her companion with her watch in her hand'), he takes possession of her in the name of his cause. He is as exploitive of Verena, therefore, as are Olive and the other characters. Not surprisingly, her tears at the end are 'not the last she was destined to shed'.

Neither Olive nor Basil are searching for the kind of order to life which James finds compatible with his needs as a writer. On the other hand, if we look again at the passage above, we see that James is no more able than his characters to place America within a structure of meaning. He begins in the urbane voice ('pretensions . . . to gentility') he uses for much of *The Bostonians*. By the middle of the passage, however, the values this voice implies have been forgotten in James's Whitman-like fascination with the cumulative details of the scene. Next, he tries tentatively ('perhaps expressive') to arrive at a meaning. Finally, he abandons the attempt, excusing himself by saying he has presented the scene 'for old acquaintance sake and that of local colour'. According to the precepts of 'The Art of Fiction', the scene should have been the setting for Basil's figure.[11] Neither James, nor his character, however, can make the connection. There is *no* connection. America is developing in a given, observed way, but ('a Dutch grocery') to what end? What is the response to make, other than one akin to Whitman's 'watching and wondering at it'?[12]

Whitman, admittedly, had some different responses (the complacently, wilfully, or genuinely celebratory) such as James does not allow himself. Even so, on one other occasion in *The Bostonians* we are reminded again of the earlier writer. It occurs during Basil's and Verena's visit to the Memorial Hall at Harvard, where the Northern dead are commemorated. During the episode we are told that Basil

> was capable of being a generous foeman, and he forgot, now, the whole question of sides and parties; the simple emotion of the old fighting time came back to him, and the monument around him seemed an embodiment of that memory; it arched over friends as well as enemies, the victims of defeat as well as the sons of triumph. (Ch. 25)

As I read these words, I am reminded especially of Whitman's 'Reconciliation'. Whitman gave the most living witness to mid-nineteenth century America, yet, darkly, even his supreme metaphor for democracy and harmony (perhaps his only real expectation of these ideals) became death. Basil, for his part, is to find in the rest of the novel no occasion for release from self equivalent even to the 'simple emotion' roused in the Memorial Hall. Nor does James discover elsewhere in *The Bostonians* anything of equal worth to the combination of 'duty and honour . . . sacrifice and example . . . youth, manhood, generosity' which he feels the memorial to the Northern dead 'speaks of'.

For James it must at times have seemed these young men

died only so that Matthias Pardon might prosper. For Basil, it must equally seem he has fought for a cause and lost everything, only so that he can come to New York and be swindled by his partner. In *The Bostonians*, as in so much American literature, we sense there is no middle ground in America between an ideal and its defeat. This is why there is rarely a coherent structure, or only the most diagrammatic structure, in American literature for adventures. Irving Howe sees James occupying in the novel a middle ground derived from a historical perspective. For James, 'the glories of Abolitionism and the Boston reform movements are a thing of the past.' His 'scepticism is that of a man who is living . . . in the backwash of a great historical moment.' Such a view certainly accords with James's proposition in *Hawthorne* that the Civil War enacted the fall of America. There is evidence to support it, moreover, in James's later account of Miss Birsdeye:

[Miss Birdseye] had always had for Olive a kind of aroma of martyrdom, and her battered, unremunerated, unpensioned old age brought angry tears, springing from the depths of outraged theory, into Miss Chancellor's eyes. For Verena, too, she was a picturesque humanitary figure. Verena had been in the habit of meeting martyrs from her childhood up, but she had seen none with so many reminiscences as Miss Birdseye, or who had been so nearly scorched by penal fires. She had had escapes, in the early days of abolitionism which it was a marvel she could tell with so little implication that she had shown courage. She had roamed through certain parts of the South carrying the Bible to the slave; and more than one of her companions, in the course of these expeditions, had been tarred and feathered. She herself, at one season, had spent a month in a Georgian jail. She had preached temperance in Irish circles where the doctrine was received with missiles; she had interfered between wives and husbands mad with drink; she had taken filthy children, picked up in the street, to her own poor rooms, and had removed their pestilent rags and washed their sore bodies with slippery little hands. In her own person she appeared to Olive and Verena as representative of suffering humanity: the pity they felt for her was part of their pity for all who were weakest and most hardly used; and it struck Miss Chancellor (more especially) that this frumpy little missionary was the last link in a tradition, and that when she could be

56

called away the heroic age of New England life—the age of plain living and high thinking, of pure ideals and earnest effort, of moral passion and noble experiment—would effectually be closed. It was the perennial freshness of Miss Birdseye's faith that had such a contagion for these modern maidens, the unquenched flame of her transcendentalism, the simplicity of her vision, the way in which in spite of mistakes, deceptions, the changing fashions of reform, which make the remedies of a previous generation look as ridiculous as their bonnets, the only thing that was still actual for her was the elevation of the species by the reading of Emerson and the frequentation of the Tremont Temple. (Ch. 20)

This account of Miss Birdseye is altogether more balanced than the earlier one, and itself calls the earlier one into question. Notice, however, that the perspective Howe gives to James is in fact given here by James only to Olive. It's Olive who sees Miss Birdseye as the last remnant of 'the heroic age of New England life'. As *we* look at the account of Miss Birdseye's 'early days', we wonder whether that age of New England life was 'heroic' or, in Howe's word, 'great'. Miss Birdseye never thinks about her courage because she never had the imagination to be afraid. Nor had she the imagination to consider that her good works might have seemed gross acts of presumption to the recipients. Her care for the children is to be praised, but her generally mindless charity is surely a 'contagion' equal to the ills it sought to remedy.

James could not believe in the perspective Howe ascribes to him. In the field, Emerson and the heroic age of New England life amounted for him to Miss Birdseye. This being said, he is left with no other perspective, and there is evidence he never had *The Bostonians* clearly in his sights. In the *Notebooks*, the novel is envisaged as a 'very *American* tale'[13] in the representative sense. What he wrote to his brother, however, is very much at odds with this ambition:

> If I have displeased people, as I hear, by calling the book *The Bostonians*—this was done wholly without invidious intention. I hadn't a dream of generalising—but thought the title simple and handy, and meant only to designate Olive and Verena by it, as they appeared to the mind of Ransom, the southerner and outsider, looking at them from New York. I didn't mean it to

cover Miss Birdseye and the others, though it might very well. I shall write another: *The Other Bostonians*.[14]

In fact, we do not believe, as we are reading *The Bostonians*, that its title is meant to prepare us for partiality, and to designate only Olive and Verena as they appear to Basil. The novel throughout shows every sign of wanting to realize the ambition of the *Notebooks* and make some general statement about America. What can indeed bother us in *The Bostonians* is that large subjects (feminism, reform movements, life in Boston and New York—all in the aftermath of the Civil War) are treated on too narrow a basis, which is yet offered with an air of complete adequacy. Such unrecognized partiality makes the satire too insistent. Unlike Dickens's, the satire is not relieved and qualified by the depiction of countless other lives that are being lived. Consequently we can sense James to be as exploitive of the novel as Olive and Basil are exploitive of Verena.

The cause of these parallel acts of exploitation is partly the same. Both the novel to James, and Verena to the other characters, reveal a minimal tendency to become anything of themselves. Both wait to be given shape and direction. Verena, in the strained times in which the novel is set can speak refreshingly for acceptance of the normal. At the end, she pleads to a cynical Basil that the nature of the people is 'fine'. Her own nature is undoubtedly of good intent: 'What *was* part of her essence was the extraordinary generosity with which she would expose herself, give herself away, turn herself inside out, for the satisfaction of a person who made demands of her' (Ch. 37). Yet such generosity, like its explicitly diseased version in Milly Theale of *The Wings of a Dove*, offers peverting temptations to acquaintances and even lovers. It leaves them with too much of Verena's fate in their hands. In turn, this places too much of their own fate in their hands. They become insufficiently conscious of, and insufficiently sustained by, anything other than the experience of the self. That this state of insufficiency is a representative fate for characters in American literature is a commonplace. Perhaps not so generally appreciated is the fact that it is also a representative fate for American writers. Characters within American works have too much on their hands because their creators, as they put the works together, are similarly overburdened. Nothing comes pre-packed in a sustaining historical and social shape to an American writer. Like Verena, the nation may take *any* shape. This blank cheque which is offered to American writers 'partly' explains their almost inevitable problems with form, structure and perspective.

It partly explains, too, James's insistent stating of *The Bostonians*. It's as if he feels compelled to impose a meaning on every moment of the novel. Intermittently, however, he becomes oppressed by his own paraded certainties. Then we meet statements such as 'I know not whether Ransom . . .' (Ch. 8), and 'Here again I must plead a certain incompetence to give an answer' (Ch. 39). With this kind of comment, James hints at adventures unrestrained by his grip on the novel. It's true the comments give us nothing to go on. They do, however, point to the James who was to write the novels that follow *The Bostonians* and *The Princess Casamassima*. In these later novels, he was to solve problems of structure by advertising the partiality and artificiality of all structures, including those of his novels. As for himself as novelist, he was to become like many modern writers increasingly elusive and invisible within the fictions so presented.

NOTES

1. *The Ambassadors*, Book 5, Chapter 3.
2. *Politics and the Novel* (New York, 1957), Chapter 7.
3. F. O. Matthiessen, *The James Family* (New York, 1948), p. 329.
4. I take this information from David Howard's essay on *The Bostonians* in John Goode (ed.), *The Air of Reality: New Essays on Henry James* (London, 1972), p. 80.
5. *The Great Tradition* (London, 1948), Chapter 3.
6. The numbers in parentheses refer to chapters from *The Bostonians*.
7. *Hawthorne* (London, 1879), Chapter 4.
8. *Hawthorne*, Chapter 2.
9. *The James Family*, p. 326.
10. My attention was drawn to this comment on Daudet by Peter Buitenhuis, *The Grasping Imagination: The American Writings of Henry James* (Toronto, 1970), p. 145.

11. David Howard notes how 'a figure is nothing without a setting' echoes 'The Art of Fiction'. *The Air of Reality*, p. 64.
12. 'Song of Myself', Chant 4.
13. F. O. Matthiessen and Kenneth B. Murdock (eds.), *The Notebooks of Henry James* (New York and London, 1961), p. 47.
14. *The James Family*, p. 329.

4

What Maisie Knew:
The Meanings that Await

I am not aware that any commentator on this novel has responded accurately to its title. Most frequently, critics change the tense of the verb, and discussion centres on what Maisie 'knows'. The implications of this change to the present tense are exemplified by Dr. Leavis, when he speaks of Maisie's 'developing awareness and understanding'.[1] 'Knows', glossed by such a phrase, is seen to have its common meaning. It signifies a developing body of knowledge derived from the past, and enabling one to function in the present in confident anticipation of the future. This body of knowledge, it is assumed, has a permanent and even transcendent status. It may grow as a body *in* time. It has also, however, an absoluteness deriving from unchanging values and is thereby the means by which time and life itself are ordered.

James's title, however, directs us to what Maisie *knew* and therefore to the finiteness of knowledge. Knowledge belonging to one time, so the title and, I would argue, the novel itself reveal, may not grow into the knowledge belonging to another time. At the beginning of Chapter 2, for example, James writes:

> In that lively sense of the immediate which is the very air of a child's mind the past on each occasion became for her as indistinct as the future: she surrendered herself to the actual

61

with a good faith that might have been touching to either parent.

These perceptive lines about the 'very air of a child's mind' (they challenge most social and parental attitudes to the behaviour and intentions of children) reveal that Maisie lives in a present, or 'actual', separated from past and future. As we read the novel, we see that the course of her life amounts to a series of reversals, in which her present may be as unprecedented by her past, as her future may be by her present. What her eventual future is, that is the one after the book finishes, we do not know. Consequently, we cannot know to what the past represented by the book has led. We ourselves, therefore, are deprived in respect to *What Maisie Knew* of a 'developing awareness and understanding'. We are left, in our response to the book, in a similar position to Maisie within the book. Our knowledge belongs to the past. It is, moreover, relative and partial, and not necessarily determinative of knowledge in the future. As the Preface tells us, in Maisie's future '(with the inevitable shift, sooner or later, of her point of view) the situation will change and become another affair, subject to other measurements and with a new centre altogether.'

In fact different meanings, even for the past, will continue to await Maisie, as they will continue to await ourselves. I adapt the title to this essay from what we are told in Chapter 1:

> it was only after some time that she was able to attach to the picture of her father's sufferings, and more particularly to her nurse's manner about them, the meaning for which these things had waited. By the time she had grown sharper, as the gentlemen who had criticised her calves used to say, she found in her mind a collection of images and echoes to which meanings were attachable—images and echoes kept for her in the childish dusk, the dim closet, the high drawers, like games she wasn't yet big enough to play.

This enactment of Maisie's position should make us aware that *What Maisie Knew* is no more to be read as a mid-nineteenth century English novel than is *Huckleberry Finn*. Unlike *David Copperfield*, *Great Expectations* and *Jane Eyre*, it does not chart a child's development to an authoritative end, where author, central character and reader meet in full recognition of what they are all supposed to know. Maisie's collection of images and echoes, like Marcel's in *In Remembrance of Things Past*, waits for whatever indeterminable meanings are 'attachable'. As for the end or structural destination of the book, it is nothing more than a natural event. We all await or have awaited it, though since it occurs at an indeterminable time it has an indeterminable meaning. In the words of the Preface, Maisie 'wonders . . . to the end, to the death—the death of her childhood'. This is an end which anticipates the one certain but again unfathomable end we all await—death itself.

Maisie's wondering parallels our own wondering on the way to death. Her representative significance in this respect, however, has not been appreciated. It's true the Preface speaks of her as an 'ironic centre', and invites us to be 'more expert critics' of her experience by taking 'advantage' of it 'better than she herself'. Most of the book's delightful comedy indeed derives from our anticipation of meanings she may eventually arrive at. This advantage over her, however, simply puts us ahead of her in time and experience, *not* ahead of her in final objectivity of knowledge or moral sense. The novel is written without benefit of the stable referents on which such knowledge or moral sense must be based. As James acknowledges in the Preface, the meanings attachable to the material of *What Maisie Knew* are sponsored entirely by its contrived point of view:

> I lose myself, truly, in appreciation of my theme on noting what she does by her 'freshness' for appearances in themselves vulgar and empty enough. They become, as she deals with them, the stuff of poetry and tragedy and art. . . . Ida Farange alone, so to speak, or Beale alone, that is either of them otherwise connected—what intensity, what 'objectivity' . . . would they have? How would they repay at all the favour of our attention?

In an earlier, *English* novel, Ida and Beale would have had the objectivity of their social position. Their station would have given them identity and function in an impersonal system larger than themselves. As in previous novels by James, and as in the major novels of Hardy his contemporary in England, this social structure no longer upholds in *What Maisie Knew*. All that can be said of society in the novel (in James's intro-

63

ductory chapter) is that it is one 'in which for the most part people [are] occupied only with chatter'. Society does not confer objectivity on its inhabitants, but, in a word taken from the above quotation from the Preface, 'appearances'.

James's use of 'appearances' argues for Maisie's representativeness for her creator, in that it reveals his own relationship to life outside the novel to be the equivalent of her relationship to life within the novel. 'Her little world', we are told, 'was phantasmagoric—strange shadows dancing on a sheet' (Ch. 1).[2] In fact James bestows on Maisie, as on many of his characters, 'the sharpened sense of spectatorship' which he was so often to claim as his own doom and passion. It gives Maisie 'an odd air of being present at her history in as separate a manner as if she could only get at experience by flattening her nose against a pane of glass' (Ch. 12). She feels 'as if she were flattening her nose upon the hard window-pane of the sweet-shop of knowledge' (Ch. 15).

This last quotation is an obvious example of the metaphorical way James renders what is the experience of a child. Nonetheless, we should understand, that insofar as life is unsubstantiated by objective referents, estranged spectatorship is a representative human condition. We will be cut off from knowledge as by a window, which may itself turn out to be a looking-glass. Through the glass may await meanings unimagined and undesired. They await Maisie, when she breaks through the glass to find her mother:

> 'My own child,' Ida murmured in a voice—a voice of sudden confused tenderness—that it seemed to her she heard for the first time. She wavered but an instant, thrilled with the first direct appeal, as distinguished from mere maternal pull, she had ever had from lips that, even in the old vociferous years, had always been sharp. The next moment she was on her mother's breast, where, amid a wilderness of trinkets, she felt as if she had suddenly been thrust, with a smash of glass, into a jeweller's shop-front, but only to be as suddenly ejected with a push and the brisk injunction: 'Now go to the Captain!' (Ch. 15)

That knowledge through the window is so unprecedented and bewildering, entails 'surrender to the actual' and the present. One is reminded of Eliot's lines in 'Burnt Norton': 'If all time is eternally present/ All time is unredeemable.' Time is eternally present and unredeemable for Maisie and all the characters in *What Maisie Knew*, because they have no perspective on time which transcends time itself. Their lives alone are the measure of their lives. Without any referents to guarantee them, they inevitably wear only a mask of life. The surface show, the performance, the parade, is everything. Beale, so the introductory chapter tells us, contrives to have 'the look of the joy of life'. Ida is soured by 'the prospect of not showing to advantage' (Ch. 3). Miss Overmore is indignant that her 'false position' (Ch. 6) may be exposed. Mrs. Wix builds her refuge 'on the firm ground of fiction' (Ch. 4). Sir Claude is conscious that his 'type' 'deceives' (Ch. 8).

Of all the characters in the book Beale alone, it seems, is too 'stupid' (Ch. 18) not to want to cast off his personal mask. He surrenders himself unresistingly, unregrettingly, to a perpetual actual. The other characters, like Maisie herself, desire desperately to be redeemed from a present having no end other than death. At one moment Ida, always created with wonderful vividness by James, is seen as an 'actress, in some tremendous situation, sweeping down to the footlights as if she would jump them' (Ch. 15). Her end may be, as an older Maisie imagines, 'madness and desolation . . . ruin and darkness and death' (Ch. 21), just because she can find no upholding reality to leap into.

In this last vision of her mother, Maisie may be looking into the face of her own unaccommodated old age. On which side of the footlights, on which side of the glass, may sustenance be found? Mrs. Wix, it seems, would like to pass Ida in mid-air in order to command a stage. As someone who has 'sidled and ducked through life' (Ch. 9), she longs to give a big performance. She eventually finds her audience in Maisie and Sir Claude:

> 'Take me, take me,' she went on and on—the tide of her eloquence was high. 'Here I am; I know what I am and what I ain't. . . . Here I am, here I am!—she spread herself into an exhibition that, combined with her intensity and her decorations appeared to suggest her for strange offices and devotions, for ridiculous replacements and substitutions. She manipulated her gown as she talked, she insisted on the items of her debt. 'I

have nothing of my own, I know . . . but my hold of this little one truth, which is all the world I can bribe you with: that the pair of you are more to me than all besides.'

This is a 'magnificent appeal' (Ch. 24), but who *does* know certainly what they are or what they ain't, or how they will be revealed? A meaning waiting to be attached to Mrs. Wix's moral passion is that ('Take me, take me') it resembles nymphomania and is probably a substitute for sexual unfulfil-ment. If carnal knowledge is something Maisie needs so that her innocence about adults may diminish, Mrs. Wix, with her warped view of sexual relationships, might be an inappro-priate mentor. She wants her 'little one truth' to be the fixed and absolute centre of all life for herself, Maisie and Sir Claude. It's challenged, however, by other truths (for example, 'amour' (Ch. 26)), which she won't take into account. Its objectivity is undermined by her parasitism and by her capacity to make-believe and self-delude. We remember that when she took Maisie to the dentist, it was she who screamed when Maisie's tooth was pulled out. Who knows too what meanings await Maisie in Mrs. Wix's stories about Clara Matilda? Has Mrs. Wix really been, as the young Maisie needs to feel, 'with passion and anguish a mother' (Ch. 4), or is this a role she plays? That motherhood may be a part to be learned, and may not come inevitably and naturally after giving birth, is evident from Ida's magnificent ignorance about it. Has there really been a Mr. Wix, whom Mrs. Wix never mentions ('save that he has been dead for ages' (Ch. 4)), and has there really been a Clara Matilda Wix? Is the grave Maisie visits labelled Clara Matilda Wix, or only Clara Matilda? James's comment that Mrs. Wix 'took refuge on the firm ground of fiction, through which indeed there curled the blue river of truth' (Ch. 4) deliberately underlines the inseparability of Mrs. Wix's truth and fiction. So do the facts (?) that 'Clara Matilda . . . was in heaven and yet, embarrassingly, also in Kensel Green' (Ch. 4).

How much Sir Claude wishes he could distinguish his own truth from his own appearance. His fear of life derives from his sense that while he has habits, he has no centre. He confesses to Maisie he married Ida, 'Just because I was afraid!' (Ch. 13). To the weak, Ida can indeed appear strong: 'She has the nerve for a tiger-shoot' (Ch. 16). To the lost, she can be as a shining beacon so that, as an older Maisie admiringly appreciates, 'it was no wonder the gentlemen were guided' (Ch. 20). Yet paradoxically Sir Claude, himself as lost as Ida, is in his turn a 'shining presence' to women. For a time, his charm can make up for any sense they share with Maisie (though more experienced and desolate than hers) of their 'fallen state' (Ch. 8). Having attracted women so easily by his surface, however, Sir Claude never knows how to relate to them otherwise. He is afraid of the lengths to which a developed relationship will take him. His protective, rehearsed formula is that 'I'm the most unappreciated of—what do you call the fellows?—family-men' (Ch. 8). As paterfamilias Sir Claude envisages for himself a role which he could believe to have objective validity. He actually likes children because with them, as with young Maisie, he feels unvulnerable. Yet (awful truth for him) he cannot have his own children unless he has a woman, and with women he feels terribly vulnerable.

All the characters in *What Maisie Knew* may wear a mask of life until they die. This sense of their plight prevents me from sharing Tony Tanner's response to the novel. As Dr. Tanner says, *What Maisie Knew* does suggest 'the relativity of all knowledge'.[3] But then he goes on to derive the following moral from the novel:

> Life will not be assessed according to *a priori* edicts, but rather by *a posteriori* inferences, and it will be loved rather than exploited. In James one is made to feel that to approach experience with a set of ethical imperatives is to mutilate life in advance. True virtue lies in opening oneself to as many as possible of the swarm of impressions which life offers, and then behaving in a manner dicated more by aesthetic unselfish considerations than by prescribed rules of conduct or perverse self-seeking. In a word, virtue is to celebrate life and to love its endless flow, not to appropriate it or attempt to arrest it—with a hand, with a code.[4]

There may be something to attract us all in this affirmation of openness. Yet it's very like a relapse into hollowness. Moreover most of the characters in *What Maisie Knew* are lost, not because they have ethical imperatives, but because they are without them. As much as Marlowe in *Heart of Darkness* they suspect that at 'the last opportunity for pronouncement [they] probably would have nothing to say.'[5] Fear of this emptiness inspires Mrs. Wix to cling dogmatically to words in the Bible. For his part, James endorses the characters' need of ethical imperatives, even though he is aware of the personal confusions and perversities prompting any one solution to it.

In fact is there not, amid all our sense of life's relativities and counterfeits, a range of ethical imperatives which we believe to centre on children? This question may become still sharper when the general grasp on values is uncertain. Residual definitions of morality may be derived from what children are allowed to know or not know, be present at or not be present at. In *What Maisie Knew* do we not actually feel the most respect for the two characters, Mrs. Wix and Sir Claude, who most try to protect Maisie? As in *The Awkward Age*, James is testing us. We may be ready to admit we have lost our objective grasp of life. Consequently, we may want to celebrate openness. But what is to happen in front of the children?

The question goes so deep as to be atavistic. Nonetheless the answers, like all the other answers we need, are shown in *What Maisie Knew* to shift bewilderingly according to time and context. Sir Claude, for example, despite his care for Maisie, has to be recognized as too ready to place what the Preface calls 'the torch of virtue' in her hand. He tells her: 'If we're not good enough for *you* . . . I'll be hanged if I know whom we shall be good enough for!' (Ch. 14). Sir Claude, as usual, says more than he knows. There is an air of desperation in this exclamation, as in his earlier, Mrs. Micawberish assertion to Maisie: 'I'll stick to you through everything' (Ch. 12). Maisie is at least the third figure in the novel on whom he's imposed the role of giving him his bearings. His self-centredness in this respect has in the past even led him into grotesque and pathetic communion during the 'hours of late evening' (Ch. 11) with Mrs. Wix.

To be good enough for Maisie leads Sir Claude to what he sees as 'the brave stroke of his getting off from Mrs. Beale as well as from his wife—of making with the child straight for some such foreign land as would give support to Mrs. Wix's dream' (Ch. 20). But for how long can he and Maisie live in Mrs. Wix's dream? As he discusses Ida with Maisie in

Boulogne, it's clear Sir Claude has a promiscuous sexual appetite which Mrs. Wix would always want to see starved:

> 'Your mother?—to South Africa? I give it up, dear boy,' Sir Claude said: and she seemed literally to see him give it up as he stood there and with a kind of absent gaze—absent, that is, from *her* affairs—followed the fine stride and shining limbs of a young fishwife who had just waded out of the sea with her basketful of shrimps. His thought came back to her sooner than his eyes. (Ch. 22)

Furthermore Maisie herself, the child for whose benefit Sir Claude is anxious to enact goodness, is changing. By the time Sir Claude brings her to Boulogne, she is becoming less of a child and may not entirely be a child any more. She takes in Sir Claude's magnetized attention to the limbs of the young fishwife. Now she is old enough, developed enough, to have intimations of what his masculine gaze might mean. She surely is by this time either immediately pre- or post-puberty. No longer can she be contained in Sir Claude's complacent and self-protective 'dear boy'.

This threatening (for Sir Claude) change in Maisie is brought home to him during his last scenes with her. Maisie makes it clear that if he will desert Mrs. Beale, she will leave Mrs. Wix:

> 'I won't even bid her good-bye,' Maisie continued. 'I'll stay out till the boat has gone. I'll go up to the old rampart.'
> 'The old rampart?'
> 'I'll sit on that bench where you see the gold Virgin.'
> 'The gold Virgin?' he vaguely echoed. But it brought his eyes back to her as if after an instant he could see the place and the thing she named—could see her sitting there alone. 'While I break with Mrs Beale?'
> 'While you break with Mrs Beale.'
> He gave her a long deep smothered sigh. 'I must see her first.'
> 'You won't do as I do? Go out and wait?'
> 'Wait?'—once more he appeared at a loss.
> 'Till they both have gone,' Maisie said.
> 'Giving *us* up?'
> 'Giving *us* up.'
> Oh with what a face for an instant he wondered if that could be! But his wonder the next moment only made him go to the

69

door and, with his hand on the knob, stand as if listening for voices. Maisie listened, but she heard none. All she heard presently was Sir Claude's saying with speculation quite choked off, but so as not to be heard in the salon: 'Mrs Beale will never go.' (Ch. 31)

According to James W. Gargano, not until 1956 'was it suggested . . . that Maisie herself is so vitiated by the evil of her "protectors" that she seeks to resolve her dilemma by offering to become Sir Claude's mistress. If it can be substantiated, this interpretation of Maisie's character would further contribute to the element of "horror" Bewley discovers in *What Maisie Knew*.'[6] Perhaps we are impoverished by not having in a case like Maisie's the firm ethical imperatives implied by Dr. Gargano's 'evil' and 'horror'. Nonetheless, he rather simplifies the possibilities of response to this poignant scene. Who knows what Maisie means by her offer to meet Sir Claude at the 'gold Virgin'? For her the venue may be no more than a convenient meeting-place. It may also, however, indicate her presumptuous desire to save Sir Claude. Immediately prior to the above exchange, when Sir Claude had failed to take the opportunity of catching a train to Paris with her, Maisie had concluded that 'Mrs Wix was right. He was afraid of his weakness.' What Mrs. Wix had actually told her, with characteristic luridness, was that Sir Claude was 'just a poor sunk slave . . . to his passions' (Ch. 29). It could be that what Maisie offers to Sir Claude is to become his virgin companion and thereby rescue him from passions whose powerful hold on him she has witnessed. Her offer could represent her determined, virginal aloofness to the threatening complications of sexual desire felt to be burgeoning even in herself.

Maisie, like any virgin, does not know what meanings await her in sexual relationships with another person. At her time of life, it is not unnatural for her to feel and even hope that, with a Sir Claude restored to a shining presence, she can live insulated from this knowledge. A dream of this kind would be one sort of innocence about life with him. Another sort, equally natural but now desirous of knowledge, is that with the chivalrous Sir Claude she could best discover the imminent meanings that await her sexually. On either terms, her offer is clearly earth-shaking for Sir Claude. Maisie now is no longer a child he can be good for, but another woman he may find on his hands.

We may feel Sir Claude shows good sense in rejecting Maisie's proposal, even though he is tempted by its tendering him yet another fresh start. Our judgement, even so, will depend as much on shifting social and psychological factors as on any we can claim to be morally absolute. Historically and from society to society, the age of consent for young girls is notoriously unfixable. As James shows in his next novel, it *is* an 'awkward age' and not one with reference to which morality can be certainly defined, even though it's an issue we want to be certain about. Sir Claude's instinct, not always praiseworthy in the past and unlikely (despite his new authority when we last see him) to be always praiseworthy in the future, caused him to refuse Maisie. Maisie, for her part, had wanted him to accept. How mysterious a quality virtue is, when the one in whose hand its torch is placed is ignorant of what she holds! All Maisie *knew* when she lost Sir Claude was 'something still deeper than a moral sense . . . she felt the rising of the tears she had kept down at the station. They had nothing— no, distinctly nothing—to do with her moral sense' (Ch. 31).

2

With its sense that its characters may wear only a mask of life, *What Maisie Knew* might have been *The Blithedale Romance* or *The Confidence Man* or *Huckleberry Finn* or *The Counterfeiters*. With its sense that its characters live as dispossessed spectators, it might have been all these other novels again or *The Mayor of Casterbridge* or *In Remembrance of Things Past*, both having many scenes in which characters gaze through windows at what they are separated from; it might too have been *The Waste Land* ('each in his prison/ Thinking of the key, each confirms a prison'). With its sense of the inevitable relativity of structures of meaning, *What Maisie Knew* relates again to any of the above works and even to *Ulysses*. At a couple of moments, it looks forward directly to Joyce's novel, for example:

> It took her some time to puzzle out with the aid of an experiment or two that it wouldn't do to talk about Mamma's youth.

71

She even went so far one day, in the presence of that lady's thick colour and marked lines, as to wonder if it would occur to any one but herself to do so. Yet if she wasn't young then she was old and this threw an odd light on her having a husband of a different generation. Mr Farange was still older—that Maisie perfectly knew; and it brought her in due course to the perception of how much more, since Mrs Beale was younger than Sir Claude, Papa must be older than Mrs Beale. Such discoveries were disconcerting and even a trifle confounding: these persons, it appeared, were not of the age they ought to be. (Ch. 10)

Maisie's reflection on the relativity of the characters' ages is reminiscent of Joyce's speculation in 'Ithaca' on the changing relations in time of Bloom's and Stephen's ages. Last of all, with its sense that the central character remains uninitiated into final knowledge, *What Maisie Knew* might have been *The Trial*. These thoughts of Maisie's, in Mrs. Wix's presence, might very well have been Joseph K's: 'Was the sum of all knowledge only to know how little in this presence one would ever reach it?' (Ch. 26).

I make these comparisons first of all to show again how James is at the meeting point of nineteenth-century American and twentieth-century European literature; secondly, to give examples of the different windows of the house of fiction through which different writers have looked at essentially similar problems. As James gazes through the window of *What Maisie Knew*, his response to what he sees is, as in so many of his works, prevailingly comic. The Preface makes it clear, however, that he might have attached darker meanings to what he looked on:

For satisfaction of the mind . . . the small expanding consciousness would have to be saved, have to become presentable as a register of impressions; and saved by the experience of certain advantages, by some enjoyed profit and some achieved confidence, rather than coarsened, blurred, sterilised, by ignorance and pain.

These words suggest that what happens to Maisie is governed more by authorial predilection than what might be said to be realistic probability. In connection with this point, Dr. Leavis's belief that '*What Maisie Knew* would pretty obviously not have been conceived by James if he hadn't read *David Copperfield*'[7] might count more against James's novel than for it. In comparison with David's, Maisie's disrupted childhood leaves her remarkably untroubled. She is bothered enough to want confirmed her intuitions about the meaning of father and mother, but there is nothing in her response to her circumstances to cause her even to be tempted to bite anyone's hand. Dr. Leavis goes on to say that *What Maisie Knew* shows 'the criteria of judgement must be the consequences for the children.'[8] In reply to this it might be argued that, if the consequences for Maisie are any guide, it might benefit all children if parents split and re-coupled as voraciously as Beale and Ida.

In other words Maisie, as the Preface recognizes, is something of a device: so much so that I am sure we all 'sometimes think', with Flannery O'Connor, that 'the child must have a bald head and a swallow-tail coat.'[9] She is a peculiar, even impossible Jamesian child. Her consciousness is her experience, her experience her consciousness. The corollary of the life James is able to conceive for her is that there are all sorts of adventures she doesn't have, which we might feel to be inevitably a part of childhood as such. Does not every child meet and associate with some other children? Would not Maisie, even if she remained separated from other children, occasionally have adventures which were not so insistently a part of the design James has for her? Why do we leave her when she is on the verge of adult adventures which James might find less containable than her childhood experience?

Such questions (and the terms 'experience' and 'adventures') lead me back to the problem I confronted in my previous chapter on *The Bostonians*. They may point to essential limitations in the amount of life James can allow his characters. The bleakest aspect of his fiction is that his characters remain unblessed by the fellow feeling and intercourse which keep most of us going to the extent that any consciousness of masked dispossession disappears. We feel connected and real. Maisie, however, with all the other characters in the book and with so many other characters in James, remains essentially unconnected. Is this why she shows as a device—because intrinsic aspects of human reality have been omitted from her case? We could answer a partial 'Yes' to this question. Then we might remember that though Maisie shows as a device more than the child David Copperfield does, she does not show as a device any more than the child Huck Finn does. Furthermore, James's and Twain's betrayal of the 'realism' of their characters is one of the points their respective novels are making. If we are dispossessed of the objective coherence which survives to uphold David, his creator, and his reader, how are we to know what are the essential aspects of human reality? What are we left with but self-exposing devices of structure and meaning? *What Maisie Knew* advertises its necessary artificiality by its symmetry and selectivity. It is *one* window in the house of fiction our world may be. Let us hope that the fellow feeling James asks us to share with him on behalf of his characters and the buoyant intercourse he offers us are at least a sign of the real thing. The life enhancement they help to enact in *What Maisie Knew* is what James wants to believe in.

NOTES

1. *Anna Karenina and Other Essays* (London, 1973), p. 82.
2. The numbers in parentheses refer to the chapters of *What Maisie Knew*.
3. *The Reign of Wonder: Naïvety and Reality in American Literature* (Cambridge, 1965), p. 288.
4. *The Reign of Wonder*, p. 298.
5. *Heart of Darkness*, Chapter 3.
6. '*What Maisie Knew*: The Evolution of a "Moral Being"', *Nineteenth-Century Fiction*, 16 (1961–62), p. 34.
7. *Anna Karenina and Other Essays*, p. 80.
8. *Anna Karenina and Other Essays*, p. 81.
9. Sally Fitzgerald (ed.), *The Habit of Being: Letters of Flannery O'Connor* (New York, 1979), pp. 332–33.

5

The Ambassadors:
Life as a False Position

> He almost blushed, in the dark, for the way he had dressed the
> possibility in vagueness, as a little girl might have dressed her
> doll. He had made them—and by no fault of their own—
> momentarily pull it for him, the possibility, out of this vague-
> ness; and must he not therefore take it now as they had had
> simply, with whatever thin attenuations, to give it to him? The
> very question, it may be added, made him feel lonely and cold.

So, at the end of Book XI, Strether responds to what has just
been revealed to him about Chad's and Madame de Vionnet's
relationship. His thoughts confirm essential alienation, unrelieved by his ambassadorial mission to Paris. He feels
estranged from the self ('a little girl' self) which dressed Chad
and Madame de Vionnet in vague idealism, even as he feels
'lonely and cold' in his dispossession of the idealism. Once
again (and like Maisie before him) what Strether has found
through the looking-glass of life has not been what he desired.
To the end, therefore, he remains where James, according to
the Preface to *The Ambassadors*, originally conceived him—in a
'false position'.

Because Strether's subjective world is unreflected by an
objective world, he is a very different hero from Dickens's
David Copperfield. In James's words from the Preface, David
in his novel is equipped with 'the double privilege of subject

and object'. One would not want to simplify David's function in *David Copperfield*, especially as the opening line of Dickens's novel warns against such a move.[1] Nonetheless it remains a fact that by the end of *David Copperfield* David, as first person narrator, has found an objective world shaped to his subjective desires. He is in a true position, and so much is publicly confirmed by his marriage to Agnes. His arrival at a true position has been an implicit destination, even destiny, throughout his long story of his life. He has told his story from the implied true position. Because of this position, Dickens, David and the reader can always know where they are.

Strether, like so many heroes of American fiction, remains unresolved and unmarried. A phase of his life arrives at a conclusion in *The Ambassadors*. The termination of the novel, however, in contrast to the termination of *David Copperfield* is not *the* end. Indeed the impossibility of reaching *the* end with Strether seems to have been one reason why James felt he could not let the character be the first person narrator of *The Ambassadors*. Unless the narrator can be imagined as fixed at the end and looking back, the first person form was all too likely for James, as he says in the Preface, to become 'the terrible *fluidity* of self-revelation'. Perhaps this phrase was written with *The Sacred Fount* in mind. Certainly, in that first person novel which immediately preceded *The Ambassadors*, we sink rather than swim in fluidity. Because it is impossible to share even an inflatable raft of security with the narrator of *The Sacred Fount*, it is impossible to establish a relationship with anything else in the novel.

Not that fluidity of self-revelation need be so terrible, even for characters as unresolved and unaccommodated as Strether. Hawthorne before James in *The Blithedale Romance*, and Proust soon after in *In Remembrance of Things Past*, show how the very substance of a first person novel can be the enactment of the narrator's fluidity of experience. Whereas David Copperfield has found himself and his true position before he writes his book, Miles Coverdale and Marcel are searching for themselves within their books in the act of writing. They remain subjective selves who may never find objectivity. Strether shares their plight, but James prefers to realize it by a method which looks forward to Joyce's stream of consciousness. *The Ambassadors*, like

Ulysses, is told from a latently authorial third person point of view, which enacts and exhibits the consciousness of the central character. I say 'latently', because the authorial point of view exists in spirit rather than substance. As exemplified in my opening quotation, in 'it may be added', James's presence in *The Ambassadors* is just short of an absence. It supports *The Ambassadors*, but it does not assign the reader to a true position with respect to the novel.

2

As I hope to show, Strether's continuing false position is a representative one for his creator. By the time of *The Ambassadors*, what James had earlier called the 'paraphernalia' of life were, as he saw them, no longer sustaining. The paraphernalia were the 'manners, usages, habits, forms'[2] by reference to which individuals and society (in literature and out of it) had established true positions. At the end of the nineteenth century, however, incongruence was in James's view the more representative fate for the individual. So 'the idea' of *The Ambassadors*, the Preface informs us, 'resides indeed in the very fact that an hour of such unprecedented ease [in Gloriani's garden] should have been felt by [Strether] *as* a crisis'. Throughout the novel, incongruities recur for Strether, as for Maisie before him: for example, the younger Chad, on whom we are never to get a fix, at first appears old to Strether and makes him feel young; Chad's claim that his relations with Madame de Vionnet are 'awfully good' compels from a conscientious Strether the question, 'Is she bad?' (V, Ch. 3)[3]; and when Sarah Pocock confronts Madame de Vionnet, who is a Countess, it appears to Strether that, of the two ladies at this moment, it is Sarah 'who most carried out the idea of a Countess' (VIII, Ch. 3).

What James in a notebook entry about *The Ambassadors* identified as 'the growing polyglot Babel'[4] expresses a generally bewildering plurality of values amid which we are all in false positions. We get the impression that in Paris, where Strether 'had never in his life heard so many opinions on so many subjects' (IV, Ch. 2), language is running away with itself. Nor is the problem confined to the talk in that city. Of his letters home, Strether wonders if they would not 'have been worthy of a showy journalist, some master of the great new science of beating the sense out of words' (VII, Ch. 3). True positions become elusive and even illusory when so much depends on the way words are used: ' "He says there's no woman", he could hear Mrs Newsome report, in capitals almost of newspaper size, to Mrs Pocock; and he could focus in Mrs Pocock the response of the reader of the journal' (IV, Ch. 2). The dependence on the way words are used is why a typical conversation in late James is one in which characters hunt for the 'word' (IV, Ch. 2). It's why also we, as readers, are often placed in the position of composing the novel with the characters as they and we go along. Even when found, words are not guaranteed to give the same signals to different parties. 'Virtuous attachment' (IV, Ch. 2), has radically different meanings for Strether and Little Bilham. Inevitably, responses are relative to personalities and to distance and time. As Strether, with typical generosity reflects: Mrs. Newsome 'couldn't at best become tactful as quickly as he. Her tact had to reckon with the Atlantic Ocean, the General Post Office, and the extravagant curve of the globe' (IV, Ch. 2).

Life is a false position when we live, not amid competing reports of the truth, but amid competing acts of the imagination from which truth may be inseparable. Like all of James's works, and like *Ulysses*, *The Ambassadors* makes many allusions to other works and notions of art alongside which it must find its place. At the end of the novel, Strether learns from Chad that even advertising is 'an art like another, and infinite like all the arts' (XII, Ch. 4). From the beginning of his conscious life, in fact, Strether has had to contend for his very identity with a name derived from a fiction—Balzac's *Louis Lambert*. His achievement, as he reflects with the kind of self-mocking, self-knowledge that always wins our affection for him, is that his identity now amounts to little more than his name being to the fore in another book of life, Mrs. Newsome's *Review*: 'He was Lambert Strether because he was on the cover, whereas it should have been, for anything like glory, that he was on the cover because he was *Lambert Strether*' (II, Ch. 2).

Strether's own sense of his possible futility makes me question the claim for him made by Richard Poirier, in one of the most significant and eloquent appreciations of *The Ambassadors*. Dr.

Poirier rightly places *The Ambassadors* in the context of American literature and implicitly relieves it of the inappropriate demands made of it by Dr. Leavis's *The Great Tradition*. Even so, given Dr. Poirier's sense of the exploratory fictionality of American literature, a surprising dogmatism sets into his conclusion about *The Ambassadors*. According to Dr. Poirier, the novel

> makes us feel that [Strether's] generosity has been betrayed by the material—like Chad—on which it has expended itself. People really ought to try to live up to such an imagination of them as Strether's—that finally is what the book asks us to believe, not anything so tiresome as that Strether has failed to be in touch with reality.[5]

Such a conclusion discounts too easily both the criticisms Strether makes of himself and also the additional criticisms we make of him. It's true that, a few pages into the novel, we are invited to see Strether 'with a vision kindly adjusted'. The invitation, however, is an advertised special plea by James, full of the knowledge that other positions in response to Strether may be equally valid. Why, we might ask, should Chad or anyone else be obliged to consider himself material for Strether's imagination? How *are* people to live up to an imagination which finds it such a strain to come to terms with sexual passion? There always was in fact a great deal of hypocrisy, which someone with Strether's capacity for self-analysis might have been expected to be aware of, in the original mission to bring Chad home to serve gods of American business regarded by Strether himself as false. As James's novels repeatedly show, no one is more capable of self-deception than those whose consciousness and imagination are most freely, and sometimes most perceptively, indulged. Incapable of confronting nineteenth-century America (his excuse is that Woollet, Mass. is 'the prison house' (II, Ch. 1)) Strether has consoled himself with personal and cultural issues which, as he suspects, might be seen as comparatively trivial: 'he had carried on at one period, in Mrs. Newsome's parlours ... a course of English literature reinforced by exams and teas' (IX, Ch. 3). He certainly has too much consciousness on other people's behalf. To Maria Gostrey he confesses that he is acting with a sense for Chad of 'Consideration and comfort and security—

the general safety of being anchored by a strong chain. He wants, as I see him, to be protected. Protected I mean from life' (II, Ch. 1). Here, Strether is manifestly using Chad as material for his imagination. But what right has he, if his own sense of failure is sincere, to protect anyone from life? What right has he to bring home Mrs. Newsome's prodigal son, be married by her, and thus reconstitute a family he has been incapable of propagating himself?

Yet regard anyone with a vision *un*kindly adjusted, and 'who shall scape whipping?' Perhaps one of the positions worth occupying, whether or not a true one, is one from which things may be seen kindly. Dr. Poirier is right in pronouncing *The Ambassadors* a 'loving book'.[6] It is full of authorial fellow feeling for Strether who, for his part (it's another reason we warm to him), wants to show fellow feeling for the other characters in the novel. We see his capacity in this respect in the last incident of Book I when Waymarsh, wandering around the old streets of Chester with Strether and Maria Gostrey, suddenly dashes into a jeweller's. The act, we read, 'had almost the note of a demonstration, and it left each of the others to show a face almost of fear'. According to Strether, Waymarsh 'has struck for freedom'. Maria responds:

> 'Ah what a price to pay! And I was preparing some for him so cheap.'
>
> 'No, no,' Strether went on, frankly amused now; 'don't call it that: the freedom *you* deal in is dear.' Then as to justify himself: 'Am I not in *my* way trying it? It's this.'
>
> 'Being here, you mean, with me?'
>
> 'Yes, and talking to you as I do. I've known you a few hours, and I've known him all my life; so that if the ease I thus take with you about him isn't magnificent'—and the thought of it held him a moment—'why it's rather base.'
>
> 'It's magnificent!' said Miss Gostrey to make an end of it. 'And you should hear,' she added, 'the ease *I* take—and I above all intend to take—with Mr Waymarsh.'
>
> Strether thought. 'About *me*? Ah that's no equivalent. The equivalent would be Waymarsh's serving me up—his remorseless analysis of me. And he'd never do that'—he was sadly clear. 'He'll never remorselessly analyse me.' He quite held her with the authority of this. 'He'll never say a word to you about me.'

She took it in, she did it justice; yet after an instant her reason, her restless irony, disposed of it. 'Of course he won't. For what do you take people, that they're able to say words about anything, able remorselessly to analyse? There are not many like you and me. It will only be because he's too stupid.' . . .

Strether still had his eyes on the jeweller's front, and he waited a moment to answer. 'He's a success of a kind that I haven't approached.'

Waymarsh's act clearly unnerves Strether and Maria. Its implication that Europe is merely a treasure-house in which Americans must assert their purchasing power undermines the more reverent pilgrimage to Europe's cultural past they want to feel they are making. Strether, however, is much less ready than is Maria simply to dispose of Waymarsh's challenge. Throughout the novel she tends to have her self-flattering and self-reassuring categories too easily available. She has lived in Europe too long to want to remember the questions Strether is prepared to ask himself. Why should the structures of Chester, and the centuries of culture they enforce, be revered by an American whose home is four thousand miles away? Why not, as an American, strike for freedom from this paraphernalia? That Waymarsh's strike in Chester may be a desperately futile gesture, that his life's strike in America has left him, as Strether sees him, in a state of 'general nervous collapse' (I, Ch. 2), does not dispose for Strether of the pressure of these questions. To accept Maria's freedom from the pressure would be, as he says, a 'dear' move, costing him much of his American identity. To exchange Waymarsh's American appeal for Maria's European appeal would need to be 'magnificent' if it were not to be 'base'. At the end, he will not marry Maria and live with her (go astray with her?) in Paris, perhaps because to do so would be too dear and not magnificent enough.

But he has some distance to travel before he reaches this decisive point. For most of the book, it seems to Strether that Europe is magnificent. In Europe, he feels he is at last meeting the requirements of his imagination and finding what might have been his true position. His life hitherto, according to his self-assessment in the Luxembourg Gardens and his speech,

'Live all you can' (V, Ch. 2), to Little Bilham at Gloriani's, has left him divided from what he considers might have been his best self. In Europe, so it is implied, this self might have found an objective place. The burden of self-doubt and subjectivity would have been eased by the continuities of meaning European civilization affords the individual. Gloriani's garden speaks to Strether of 'survival, transmission, association, a strong indifferent persistent order', in which, in striking contrast to the American continent, even the open air is 'all a chamber of state' (V, Ch. 1). Madame de Vionnet's house expresses 'the peace of intervals, the dignity of distances and approaches' amid which 'the mistress of the scene before him, beautifully passive under the spell of transmission . . . had only received, accepted and been quiet' (VI, Ch. 1).

The sustenance Strether believes European traditions provide is undoubtedly what James himself came to Europe for and what, according to *The American Scene* (1907), he could still miss in America during his final visit to his native land. Eliot too, in 'Tradition and the Individual Talent' (1919), and in *Notes Towards the Definition of Culture* (1948), was later to argue for the advantages of what Strether identifies as 'a strong indifferent persistent order'. What has happened to Chad's individual talent, as Strether sees it, is very close to the benefits Eliot believed tradition afforded the individual poet and by implication the individual as such. Chad's energy has been given coherence and meanings: 'he had formerly, with a great deal of action, expressed very little; and he now expressed whatever was necessary with almost none at all' (IV, Ch. 1). For the American Strether it is as if his younger compatriot has found in Europe what their nation unendingly and inescapably seeks: that is, as James later put it, 'the word, the *fin mot*, of what it may mean.'[7]

At Gloriani's gathering, however, it is apparent that the Europe Strether sees is the one he imagines. He is convinced he has found in reality what he has always believed in and longed for. His anxiety that the occasion should be momentous is evident in his interpretation of his meeting with Gloriani as a 'trial . . . a test of his stuff' (V, Ch. 1). There is actually no sign in the encounter that Strether is of anything more than the most fleeting interest to Gloriani. He is indeed in a false position in making his declaration, 'Live all you can', at this gathering. Little, it seems, would those assembled care for what is best in Strether himself, his fundamental conscientiousness of purpose, his wondering, as Stephen Dedalus will later, 'was that only possible which came to pass'. It is in part out of Little Bilham's own sense of futility if such occasions are to represent his own fate that he assures Strether, 'I don't know that I want to be, at your age, too different from you' (V, Ch. 2). Gloriani to us appears still the operator he was in *Roderick Hudson*. Far from being upheld by the impersonal traditions in which Strether accommodates him, Gloriani ('with a personal lustre almost violent') may embody an energy undirected by anything other than itself. With 'his genius in his eyes, his manners on his lips' (V, Ch. 1), he may be entirely without centre. Later, less thrilled by Gloriani's presence, Strether himself senses the artist's 'charming hollow civility' (VI, Ch. 2).

For her part, Madame de Vionnet's position, as she knows, is at least as false as Strether's. When he first visits her and imagines her 'beautifully passive under the spell of transmission', he actually finds her seated on 'a small stuffed and fringed chair, one of the few modern articles in the room'. While Strether sits opposite, she is not 'to shift her posture by an inch' (VI, Ch. 1). Unsuspected by Strether, Madame de Vionnet is always a woman living at the very edge of her resources. Her visit to the church, when she reminds a habitually authorial Strether of 'some fine firm concentrated heroine of an old story' (VII, Ch. 1), is surely a vain recourse to traditional solace. Her account of hers and Chad's relationship (to Strether 'a high fine friendship' (VI, Ch. 3)) is: 'I don't go about with him in public' (VII, Ch. 1).

Dr. Leavis then revealed the insufficiency of his own inquiry into *The Ambassadors* when he asked:

> What . . . is this, symbolized by Paris, that Strether feels himself to have missed in his own life? Has James himself sufficiently inquired? Is anything adequately realized? If we are to take the elaboration of the theme in the spirit in which we are meant to take it, haven't we to take the symbol too much at the glamorous face-value it has for Strether?[28]

To Strether's American imagination, and to many other imaginations looking for a cultural home and a perspective on their lives, *The Ambassadors* makes it very clear what Paris symbolizes. It also makes it clear what Paris symbolizes to a different imagination like Jim Pocock's. Nor do we have to take the 'symbol at the glamorous face-value it has for Strether'. James sees in his creative work what Eliot also presents in *The Waste Land*: European structures he himself has valued are disintegrating. Europe by the end of the nineteenth century is, as America has been since its creation, without upholding order. Worn out, it needs (as Madame de Vionnet needs even Chad) new forces of vitality. Moreover the European problem (still with us) may be more complicated than the American. In America, the search for the *fin mot* is amid space and blankness. In Europe it lies hidden in so many confusing, overlapping layers of earlier structures.[9] Dr. Leavis makes it sound as if it ought to be only too easy to say what Paris means. Yet the city, a creation of so much history and art, surely meets everyone's imagination more than half way. The common experience of even a day trip to Paris is surely Strether's: 'wherever one paused . . . the imagination reacted before one could stop it' (II, Ch. 2). In this inevitable false position, how is one to say what Paris is?

Strether's awareness of how Paris enthralls the imagination reminds us again that his blindness on other occasions is, paradoxically, that of a man well-equipped with perception. When the second party of Mrs. Newsome's ambassadors arrives, no one could make a better assessment of his position than he makes himself. As he rides with Jim Pocock from the station, he wonders why none of the new arrivals has commented on Chad's improvement:

> Was he, on this question of Chad's improvement, fantastic and away from the truth? Did he live in a false world, a world that had grown simply to suit him, and was his present slight irritation—in the face now of Jim's silence in particular—but the alarm of the vain thing menaced by the touch of the real? Was this contribution of the real possibly the mission of the Pococks?—had they come to make the work of observation, as *he* had practised observation, crack and crumble, and to reduce Chad to the plain terms in which honest minds could deal with

him? Had they come in short to be sane where Strether was destined to feel that he himself had only been silly?

He glanced at such a contingency, but it failed to hold him long when once he had reflected that he would have been silly, in this case, with Maria Gostrey and Little Bilham, with Madame de Vionnet and little Jeanne, with Lambert Strether, in fine, and above all with Chad Newsome himself. Wouldn't it be found to have made more for reality to be silly with these persons than sane with Sarah and Jim? (VIII, Ch. 2)

Strether's position at this moment is classically representative of anyone who feels he possesses a superior view. In the end, what can one do but believe it *is* a superior view and have confidence in the structure of relations which seems to support it?

In our false position, however, the view creates the structure, the structure the view. Strether, who has been informed by Little Bilham that he is 'not a person to whom it's easy to tell things you don't want to know' (V, Ch. 1), can be as impervious as any of us to signals which do not fit his view. We see this in the following scene when, convinced himself of Jim Pocock's mere vulgarity of appetite in Paris, he tells Madame de Vionnet:

'Jim's intensely cynical.'

'Oh dear Jim!' Mme. de Vionnet vaguely smiled.

'Yes, literally—dear Jim! He's awful. What *he* wants, heaven forgive him, is to help us.'

'You mean'—she was eager—'help *me?*'

'Well, Chad and me in the first place. But he throws you in too, though without as yet seeing you much. Only, so far as he does see you—if you don't mind—he sees you as awful.'

' "Awful"?'—she wanted it all.

'A regular bad one—though of course of a tremendously superior kind. Dreadful, delightful, irresistible.'

'Ah dear Jim! I should like to know him. I *must.*'

'Yes naturally. But will it do? You may, you know,' Strether suggested, 'disappoint him.'

She was droll and humble about it. 'I can but try. But my wickedness then,' she went on, 'is my recommendation for him?'

'Your wickedness and the charms with which, in such a degree as yours, he associates it. He understands, you see, that

Chad and I have above all wanted to have a good time, and his view is simple and sharp. Nothing will persuade him—in the light, that is, of my behaviour—that I really didn't, quite as much as Chad, come over to have one before it was too late.' (IX, Ch. 1)

How perceptive Jim is about Strether's latent motive for coming to Paris. Not surprisingly, though Strether is surprised, we learn soon after the above exchange that Madame de Vionnet and Jim are out on the town together. Despite Strether's doubts, which delight us, she is sure she knows how not to disappoint Jim. She is capable of being at least as cynical as Strether claims Jim to be. If it will help her to keep possession of Chad, she will string this new ambassador along just as, in the above scene ('she was droll'), we see her stringing the old ambassador along.

Madame de Vionnet's response to her own position is truer than Strether's to his, to the extent that she is aware she has no position. From her point of view, Sarah Pocock is undoubtedly better placed than herself. Her envy of Sarah is evident as she and Strether continue to discuss the second party of ambassadors. Strether asserts confidently:

'Oh, "do what they will"—! They won't do much; especially if Sarah hasn't more—well, more than one has yet made out— to give.'
Madame de Vionnet weighed it. 'Ah she has all her grace!' It was a statement over which, for a little they could look at each other sufficiently straight, and though it produced no protest from Strether the effect was somehow as if he had treated it as a joke. (XI, Ch. 1)

For Madame de Vionnet, even Sarah's grace is no joke. Later in the scene she adds, 'I lost myself in *her*.' Separated from her husband, burdened by a daughter of marriageable age, victim of a passion for a younger, footloose man, Madame de Vionnet knows that all the advantages are Sarah's. Faced by Sarah, she stands, in her own eyes, completely unmasked.

So we arrive at the crux of the novel. How do we decide between Sarah Pocock's and Strether's positions with respect to Chad's and Madame de Vionnet's relationship? Not to understand the liaison as an adulterous one, and even as a re-enactment of original sin, may cut one loose from whatever values and certainties remain. Sarah, therefore, feels compelled to react to Madame de Vionnet very much as her New England ancestors in *The Scarlet Letter* respond to Hester Prynne: 'Do you consider her', she asks Strether, 'even an apology for a decent woman?' (X, Ch. 3).

Her response, which has the inherited weight of New England Calvinism behind it, cannot be summarily dismissed. Sarah is at least without the shallowness of her husband who, in words from *The Scarlet Letter*, can 'find only a theme for jest in an exhibition like the present'. All the edge will be lost from the marvellous scene in Book VIII, Chapter 3, when Madame de Vionnet beautifully 'shops' Strether, if it is not understood it must be the first occasion Sarah has knowingly opened her doors to a 'scarlet' lady. But though Sarah can lay claim to a moral posture which, in Madame de Vionnet's eyes, allows her 'all her grace', her position too is false. Her heated display of moral outrage to Strether is no more than a self-serving mask of belief. It betrays wilfulness rather than sincerity. She may well, like Strether, see Madame de Vionnet as Cleopatra. In doing so, she also sees Paris as the subverting Egypt to New England's Rome, where women like herself are as Caesar. Madame de Vionnet has released the 'hideous' (X, Ch. 3) Antony in Chad and, as Chad knows, Sarah 'hates' (XI, Ch. 1) this in a man. Sarah herself has a marriage according to Woollet, Massachusetts in which the men earn the money and occasionally break loose and run a little wild, while the women ensure that in life's inevitable expiation things don't fall apart. She can only have married Jim in despair of fulfilment with a man, and even in despair of happiness in life as such. The curious fact that she returns Madame de Vionnet's visit contributes to our sense of the essential bleakness of her own position. The event surely signals more than the obligations of good manners. It suggests how much Sarah lost something of *herself* in Madame de Vionnet's presence. What is it about Madame de Vionnet, Sarah must have asked herself, that makes men want her? Because of, not despite, this self-doubt, Sarah must emphatically describe Strether's version of events as 'an outrage to women like *us*' (X, Ch. 3). To conclude otherwise would be too great a personal challenge for her to bear.

87

Sarah's view of Chad and Madame de Vionnet suits *her* book, but her book is neither truer nor falser than anyone else's in *The Ambassadors*. Our false position, as James exhibits it, is a double bind. Either we only find what we seek in the looking-glass, or we don't find what we seek. In neither case are we equipped, like David Copperfield, 'with the double privilege of subject and object'. If we can be sure Strether eventually learns anything from his experience in Paris, it is a lesson of this kind. Paradoxically enough, he has been spending his time in the old world as if he were in the Garden of Eden, where the word was always one with the object. It is appropriate, therefore, that his disillusion should occur when he becomes aware of the sexual nature of Chad's and Madame de Vionnet's liaison. Yet though he feels immediately 'lonely and cold' in his dispossession of his make-believe, within a short time we read:

> it herewith pressed upon him that their eminent 'lie', Chad's and hers, was simply after all such an inevitable tribute to good taste as he couldn't have wished them not to render . . . once more and yet once more, he could trust her. That is he could trust her to make deception right. (XII, Ch. 2)

This conviction amounts to an immense Pandora's box of problems about the relation between taste, deception and reality. Whereas Strether, as we leave him, is only beginning to lift the lid of the box, his creator has been displaying its contents throughout *The Ambassadors*. Strether, however, is living in a world James is creating. To this extent author has advantage over character. No more than the rest of us can Strether remain contemplative and stop his life until everything is clear. No more than the rest of us can he continue to remember he may not have anything clear.

Contrary to his trust in her, the Madame de Vionnet Strether meets for the last time is hardly finding it possible to make anything right. She talks nervously, off the top of her head, saying what she wishes she *could* believe: 'What it comes to is that it's not, that it's never, a happiness, any happiness at all, to *take*. The only safe thing is to give' (XII, Ch. 2). The James who twenty years earlier had depicted the dark consequences of Ralph Touchett's giving, and who was very soon to

write of the equally black outcome of Milly Theale's bene-
ficence, surely did not intend us to respond, as Tony Tanner[10]
does, uncritically to these words. How could Madame de
Vionnet, with her passion, *not* be a taker? How could she live
in Strether's book? Unlike Strether, she has always appreciated
the difference between Miss Barrace's 'wonderful', when used
of herself, and Strether's own. Now, momentarily sentimental,
she wishes Strether's were the true one: 'it's only that you
don't snub me, as you've had fifty chances to do.' What a false
position she remains in! She has not got Strether himself right:
'You know so, at least,' she tells him, 'where you are!'

Even as he faces her, Strether is struggling to maintain
whatever bearings he has. At this stage in his life, he can still
marvel and be alarmed that sexual passion has such a hold on
Madame de Vionnet. Again we remember the pale figure of
his wife who, apparently unwarmed by her husband, died so
young. Now, at 55, Strether may understand, but may never
experience, the fact that sexual passion between human beings,
occasions the commonest and perhaps the greatest make-
believe. One wonders if he even appreciates the sexual implications of his last words to Madame de Vionnet. By this stage,
she has recovered something of her resilience, but to her pro-
vocative confession of the voraciousness of her desire ('I want
everything. I've wanted you too') Strether declares at the
door: 'Ah but you've *had* me!' He has, recognizably, been had
as he understands having. Madame de Vionnet has taken
from him the very best of his imagination. With her he has
indeed enjoyed 'an amount of experience out of any proportion
to his adventures' (V, Ch. 3). Though he has gained riches in
experience, however, the comparative poverty of his adventures
remains undiminished. How much is left out of his sense of
being had and of having! What a final, though unintentional,
cruelty his last words are to Madame de Vionnet. They cast
her passion, and all she has at stake on it, into oblivion.

It is important to understand to the end that James's
exhibition of Strether is critical as well as loving. To do so
prevents one from too easily identifying James with Strether's
'renunciation',[11] or from alleging against James, what might
be alleged against Strether: 'a pervasive sense of the danger
inherent in experience as such', so that James himself becomes

'an appreciative but apprehensive spectator'.[12] The renunciation issue is usually provoked by Strether's refusal in the closing pages of Maria Gostrey's offer of marriage. This last episode, however, is completely, if ambiguously, placed by the author. On the one hand, Strether has positive cause not to accept Maria. His view of life always more complicated than hers, he has now outgrown the succour and guidance she earlier provided. In the last Book, he shows *her* round Paris. Not surprisingly, therefore, on behalf of 'what I can make of it', he rejects her 'selection' of a life, even a life that 'built him softly round . . . and roofed him warmly over'. On the other hand, Strether's refusal of Maria demonstrates too his undiminished commitment to his own absoluteness. Like many characters in American literature, he ultimately finds himself unable to accept any accommodation. The false position is finally accommodation as such. Rather than this compromise, Strether will face even the prospect of no position at all.

Any questions James prompts us to ask about Strether's visions must be questions James also, as a lifetime writer and indulger of his own imagination, asked about his own. When we remember too that James was a lifetime bachelor, parallels between author and character may seem irresistibly to converge. But James is to be positively distinguished from Strether. Strether's imagination is revealed as too singular and absolute. James's is plural. While people can find it impossible to live in Strether's book, they are living vividly in James's. And if, as for every character in the novel, ambassadorship in a foreign place is our inevitable false position, no literary critic's response to this fate will outvie that of a writer of James's achievement. How can a novelist of his productiveness not be recognized to have put himself boldly on offer to the world? No wonder he understands everything about Madame de Vionnet. What a passion was his for intercourse with us.

NOTES

1. For a full discussion of the narrator of *David Copperfield* see the essays by Keith Carabine, Mark Kinkead-Weekes and Stephen Lutman in Ian Gregor (ed.), *Reading the Victorian Novel: Detail into Form* (London, 1980).

2. See James's letter of 31 January 1880 to W. D. Howells.
3. The numbers in parentheses refer to the Books and Chapters of *The Ambassadors* as published in *The Novels and Tales of Henry James* (New York, 1909). The first Roman numeral indicates the Book.
4. F. O. Matthiessen and Kenneth B. Murdock (eds.), *The Notebooks of Henry James* (New York and London, 1961), p. 378.
5. *A World Elsewhere: The Place of Style in American Literature* (London, New York, 1968), p. 136.
6. *A World Elsewhere*, p. 131.
7. *The American Scene* (London, 1907), pp. 114–15.
8. *The Great Tradition* (London 1948), Chapter 3.
9. Elsa Nettels observes: 'during the nineteenth century France passed through more different clearly defined phases, and existed under more different forms of government, than any other important European country. In *The Ambassadors* allusions are made to at least six different periods.' '*The Ambassadors* and the Sense of the Past', *Modern Language Quarterly*, 31 (1970), 220–35.
10. 'The Watcher from the Balcony: Henry James's *The Ambassadors*', *Critical Quarterly*, 8 (1966), 35–52.
11. As J. A. Ward does in '*The Ambassadors* as a Conversion Experience', *The Southern Review*, 5 (1969), 350–74.
12. 'The Watcher from the Balcony.'

6

The Wings of the Dove: The Mere Aesthetic Instinct of Mankind

1

He hadn't only never been near the facts of her condition which counted so as a blessing for him; he hadn't only, with all the world, hovered outside an impenetrable ring fence, within which there reigned a kind of expensive vagueness made up of smiles and silences and beautiful fictions and priceless arrangements, all strained to breaking; but he had also, with everyone else, as he now felt, actively fostered suppressions which were in the direct interest of every one's good manner, every one's pity, every one's really quite generous ideal. It was a conspiracy of silence, as the *cliché* went, to which no one had made an exception, the great smudge of mortality across the picture, the shadow of pain and horror, finding in no quarter a surface of spirit or of speech that consented to reflect it. 'The mere aesthetic instinct of mankind—!' our young man had more than once, in the connection said to himself; letting the rest of the proposition drop, but touching again thus sufficiently on the outrage even to taste involved in one's having to *see*. So then it had been—a general conscious fool's paradise, from which the specified had been chased like a dangerous animal. (IX, Ch. 4)[1]

Such is Merton Densher's assessment of his and the others' response to Milly Theale's case. As with Strether in *The Ambassadors* and several previous James characters, events

92

force Densher to question to what extent his life has been larger for his taste.[2] Necessarily, this question had long preoccupied James himself, since he early conceived his own life as very much an aesthetic enterprise. 'To be an American', he wrote to Thomas Sergeant Perry in September 1867, 'is an excellent preparation for culture . . . we can deal freely with forms of civilisation not our own, can pick and choose and assimilate and (aesthetically &C) claim our property where we find it.'

Several of James's novels, including *The Wings of the Dove*, present an American composing his or her life in this way. At the same time, his works show that the momentous fate announced in the letter was not to remain exclusively American. The requirement to be prepared for culture becomes pressing in the old world too, as Europeans find themselves separated from what might earlier have sustained them. If the traditional co-ordinates of reality no longer uphold, estrangement, which was also part of what it was to be an American searching for cultural accommodation, becomes a more general human condition. Milly Theale's exile finds parallels in Kate's and Densher's in *The Wings of the Dove*, in Tess's in *Tess of the D'Urbervilles*, and Bloom's in *Ulysses*.

In 1867, the young James could write of existing 'forms of civilisation'. By the time of *The Wings of the Dove*, these forms have become in Lord Mark's words, 'the vague billows of some great greasy sea in mid-Channel' (IV, Ch. 1). With reference to what, therefore, was any one life to be composed? The question is as immediate for a novelist as for the characters in his novel. As much as the characters in *The Wings of the Dove*, as much as Hardy with Tess and Joyce with Bloom, as much as Milly herself, James is asking *himself* which are the appropriate words for Milly. Is she Mrs. Stringham's 'princess', Kate's 'dove', the Psalmist's dove,[3] Densher's American girl, Lord Mark's woman in the Bronzino portrait; or is she at different times either her own independent composition, or her own assimilation of these roles? Furthermore, what is the significance of the 'aesthetic instinct' in the achievement of appropriate words for Milly, or for anyone or anything else? Before the 'great greasy sea', before the 'great smudge of mortality', it may be that no one instinct, or idea of order, has any claim to

93

pre-eminence. If 'every one's good manner, every one's pity, every one's really quite generous ideal' are only at best another of the 'beautiful fictions', why not with Kate frankly manipulate them as fiction? Even her creator, in the Preface of the novel, claims no intrinsic moral pre-eminence for the 'aesthetic instinct'. 'The enjoyment of a work of art, the acceptance of an irresistible illusion', he writes, '[constitutes], to my sense, our highest experience of "luxury".'

The characters in *The Wings of the Dove* belong, in words from the Preface, to 'communities of doom'. They fail to find a transcendent or impersonal cause for being or doing anything. Nor can they meet one another on any reassuring middle ground of mutual understanding. They and their world are realized by James from deep fellow feeling. He is confronting in his characters a dispossession which may be his own, and in which his own aesthetic instinct may be 'mere'. Whether or not these two possibilities become the case is for the individual reader to judge. For many, Edith Wharton's pronouncement about late James will always say enough. With her, they will find the later novels to be 'severed from that thick nourishing human air in which we all live and move'.[4]

Other readers will question with James whether the human air of itself inevitably is thick and nourishing. The 'medal', to which in the Preface James likened *The Wings of the Dove*, is a medal commemorating the dubiousness of every motion made by the characters. How then are they to realize 'the sincerities, the lucidities, the utilities', 'that blessedly, as is assumed, *might* be', which could be a source of relief? I take these quoted words from the Preface to 'The Lesson of the Master'. There, James asserts that these ideals are what 'applied irony' in fiction always campaigns for. *The Wings of the Dove* is replete with 'applied irony', enabling us to make more of everything in the novel than do the characters themselves. Nonetheless, the needed 'sincerities', 'lucidities', and 'utilities' remain elusive. Neither the characters nor we are pointed to lessons to be learned. Rather, as I shall show, the meanings of the face side of the medal are never the meanings of the reverse side. One version of 'that blessedly, as is assumed, *might* be' (envisaged, for example, in Densher's intentions towards Milly) promotes disaster. In response to this bleakness, we can still insist with

Edith Wharton that, away from *The Wings of the Dove* and late James generally, the human air *is* thick and nourishing. James, however, with an aesthetic the very opposite of 'mere', convinces us of a less reassuring possibility.

2

I shall now consider in turn Milly, Kate and Densher, and their effect on one another. What I have already said should have begun what I hope the rest of this chapter will complete: that is the unsettling of the general consensus of agreement among critical approaches to *The Wings of the Dove*. This consensus enables John Goode, in a recent essay, to be very confident about what he calls the novel's 'Parabolic direction' and 'Moral fable', and to assert that 'there doesn't seem to be much room for varying interpretations.'[5] According to this consensus,[6] Milly Theale is a Christ-like martyr, who 'rejects every lure that the world can offer and determines that the best mode of expressing her love for mankind and her forgiveness for its selfishness and greed is to die for it.'[7] Merton Densher's alleged experience of this process 'has to have representative value',[8] and his and our reward from the novel is 'a variety of religious experience'.[9]

Such a firm consensus is surprising, not only in view of Milly's and Densher's own infirmity of purpose and understanding, but also because the Preface to *The Wings of the Dove* indicates the novel is not intended to be so straightforwardly read. In the Preface James says: 'could I but make my medal hang free, its obverse and its reverse, its face and its back, would beautifully become optional for the spectator.' Moreover, one of the options he directs our attention towards is Milly's own culpability. He recognizes that although 'the main dramatic complication [is] much more prepared *for* [Milly] than by her', her own hands are nonetheless 'imbrued'; so much so, that we watch the surrounding characters drawn to her, 'as by some pool of a Lorelei—see them terrified and tempted and charmed; bribed away, it may even be, from more prescribed and natural orbits, inheriting from their connection with her strange difficulties and still stranger opportunities.'

95

The Wings of the Dove needs to be rescued from the ethereal realms to which it has been consigned by critics carried away by Densher's 'transcendent motions' (IX, Ch. 1). We should remember that in James any character's consciousness is only authoritative when no other options are available to us. We first come across Milly, for example, in the company of Mrs. Stringham's consciousness of her. Mrs. Stringham, we have been told, is from Burlington, Vermont. She is a writer of short stories, and 'she fondly believed she had her "note", the art of showing New England without showing it wholly in the kitchen.' 'She honestly believed that she was . . . supremely equipped for leading Milly's own [life].' Such is the 'mere aesthetic instinct' of Mrs. Stringham, that imagines the Milly in the Alps as someone 'looking down on the kingdoms of the earth' (III, Ch. 1).

Even though Mrs. Stringham's consciousness of Milly is 'placed' by James, the scene in the Alps has nonetheless pointed in an irresistible direction, for those who want to see Milly as a Christ figure. As Millicent Bell observes, 'Everyone has seen here a suggestion of Christ's temptation in the desert', the outcome of which is Christ's refusal 'to renounce his humanity'. Dr. Bell continues: 'His divinity, so available, must wait for its ultimate manifestation when the ultimate in human suffering has been reached. Milly has emulated Christ resolving at this moment to embrace "the whole assault of life", "the full predicament" of being human—not her princely power of wealth nor her imminent death exempt her from what this readiness entails.'[10]

Despite the reference to 'the full predicament of being human', such an interpretation has the effect, as do the characters' idealizations of Milly, of diminishing her humanity. Even the language of the analogy with Christ becomes self-evidently too grandiose and remote from common mortality. Christ is tempted by Satan to demonstrate and affirm his godliness in worldly terms, but by what along these lines can Milly ever be enticed? Her possibilities exist always on the scale of human limitation, not divine omnipotence. This is why the analogy with the Biblical scene will not fit. The Alps are not the Holy Land, and as a puzzled F. O. Mathiessen commented, 'at no point in the novel does [James] want to suggest that [Milly] is tempted by the devil in her choice of the world.'[11] So tenuous perhaps is Milly's hold on life when we first meet her, she is already beginning to wonder if life's most legitimate temptations may ever come her way. And *if* she is rejecting suicide at this moment, it's not, as Mrs. Stringham presumes, because she knows herself 'unmistakably reserved for some more complicated passage', for 'taking full in the face the whole assault of life'. How can Milly have such confident expectations? Immediately after the scene on the promontory of rock, she reveals obliquely that the problem she has just been facing there with regard to her life is 'Shall I have it for long? That is if I *have* got it' (III, Ch. 2). Her only knowledge as she allegedly looks down on 'the kingdoms of the earth', is that she may be reserved for the bleak simplicity of an early death; the one permitted complication being how to face a dispossession so final, and against which her commanding wealth may be as nothing.

Why was James so long possessed, as he confesses in the Preface, by the 'idea . . . of a young person, conscious of a great capacity for life, but early stricken and doomed, condemned to die under short respite, while also enamoured of the world?' Why did he feel, as he goes on to say, that such a young person, for full development of the idea must be American? 'To be the heir of all the ages only to know yourself as that consciousness should deepen, balked of your inheritance' possessed James as a peculiarly American fate.

My speculations prompt me to the option of relating Milly, who is to die young, to other central characters in American literature (Ishmael and Huck, for example) who remain incapable of adulthood. Their fate and Milly's is also classically expressed in Whitman's poem, 'There was a child went forth.' In this poem, too, the child never grows up. All things, the poem concludes, 'became part of that child who then went forth every day, and who now goes, and will always go forth every day'. Every day, prepared for culture, the child goes forth, devouring experience and therefore rendering it endlessly transient; never settling into adulthood, never convinced of what is real: 'whether that which appears so is so, or is it all flashes and specks?' Death is the only certainty in the poem's self-conscious show of life.

Death has become the only certainty for Milly too, as she wonders what only an American, 'heir to all the ages', and positively charged with 'life, liberty and the pursuit of happiness', could have the presumption to wonder: 'If I've got everything' (III, Ch. 2). Theoretically, the world has always been before her. She remains darkly conscious, however, of having 'lived all these years as if I were dead', and of imminently dying 'as if I were alive' (IV, Ch. 3). To her too, we surmise, the world has remained, as it did to Whitman's child, 'all flashes and specks'. There has been no assuring structure of reality and growth. Her family's history has culminated in self-doubt and self-destruction, leaving her 'a survivor of a general wreck' (IV, Ch. 33). It is a story of New York which James's later visit to the city was to confirm. In *The American Scene* he was to write of New York: 'the very sign of its energy is that it doesn't believe in itself; it fails to succeed, even at a cost of millions, in persuading you that it does.'[12]

Like the previous American heroes and heroines of her creator, Milly finds nothing in Europe to take her life out of her hands and convince her of its significance and substantiality. From Lord Mark and Sir Luke Strett (both emphatically secular) she learns respectively these gospels 'Nobody here, you know, does anything for nothing' (IV, Ch. 1); and 'when I talk of life I think I mean more than anything else the beautiful show of it' (VII, Ch. 2). How can she, as Sir Luke advises, live 'by option, by volition' (V, Ch. 4)? As an American, she knows more than her doctor ever will about the void awaiting commitment to this prescription. No wonder she reverses his advice. As she gazes at the Londoners in Regent's Park, she concludes:

> They could live if they would; that is, like herself, they had been told so: she saw them all about her, on seats, digesting the information, recognising it again as something in a slightly different shape familiar enough, the blessed old truth that they would live if they could.

Later in the chapter she thinks again: 'It was perhaps superficially more striking that one could live if one would; but it was more appealing, insinuating, irresistible in short, that one would live if one could' (V, Ch. 4).

Such reassurance as Milly does find lies in the sense that life is always against the odds. This conviction may be inevitable in someone so convinced of imminent death that at Matcham she can say, with reason, 'I shall never be better than this' (V, Ch. 2). Even so, as we consider the face and back of James's medal, we can see that Milly's transformation of the doctor's advice amounts to a characteristic presumptuousness on her part. So anxious is she not to evade recognition of her 'ultimate state', she becomes rather too self-congratulatory: Sir Luke 'hadn't known—how could he—that she was devilishly subtle, subtle exactly in the manner of the suspected, the suspicious, the condemned' (V, Ch. 4). The whole course of the novel is to show that Milly, confronted by roles the aesthetic instincts of others create for her, needs her subtlety for self-preservation. Yet her *devilish* subtlety fabricates in its turn a self-serving theatre of experience. In this theatre, for example, Mrs. Stringham is 'Susan Shepherd', her doctor her patient ('him too she would help to help her' (VII, Ch. 2)), the people in Regent's Park, who are likely to have their own views on life, a confirmation of her personal fate. Milly diagnoses in Kate 'a sort of failure of common terms' (IV, Ch. 3), but she herself fails also of such terms. Separated from the vanity of human wishes as only the condemned may be, she becomes too absolute unto the self, too resistant to an approach. She tells Lord Mark: 'I give and give and give . . . Only I can't listen or receive or accept—I can't *agree*. I can't make a bargain' (VII, Ch. 4). Only the re-entry of Densher into her world disturbs her absoluteness. Apart from with him, she remains as unavailable for ordinary human relationships as ever Kate is. She therefore presents the others with their 'strange difficulties and stranger opportunities'. She is complicitous in 'the mere aesthetic instinct of mankind' which promotes 'a general conscious fool's paradise'. Human intercourse has manifestly been aborted, when it's only to someone one little cares about (in Milly's case, Lord Mark), that one can frankly reveal: 'I'm very badly ill' (VII, Ch. 4).

I want now to turn to Kate and Densher, to Milly's effect on them and theirs on Milly. Our first meeting with Kate, as she gazes into the mirror in her father's room and then looks out from his windows, anticipates our first encounter with Milly.

The English girl too is introduced as someone without an objective place in the world and therefore in a state of perched alienation. Like Milly, Kate also has behind her, for a family history, an aborted composition:

> the whole history of their house had the effect of some fine florid voluminous phrase, say even a musical, that dropped first into words and notes without sense and then, hanging unfinished, into no words nor any notes at all. (I, Ch. 1)

We meet Kate in her position of aloof unrelatedness again in the novel's second chapter, as she looks out from her aunt's windows. Her lover too shares her plight. Since their first meeting, she and Densher 'had remained confronted on their ladders' (II, Ch. 1).

As we begin the novel, Kate has an option on one of three prescribed and perhaps natural orbits. She can stay with her aunt and reward Mrs. Lowder's 'investment' in her with the 'interest' of Lord Mark; she can marry Densher; she can give up her life to her father. When we first meet her, she has come to her father to escape her aunt and to try to find an identity for herself as a daughter. She is indeed as anxious it be recognized she has offered herself for this filial role, as she is incredulous her life has come to this hopeless pass: 'I wish there were someone here who might serve—for any contingency—as a witness that I *have* put it to you that I'm ready to come' (I, Ch. 1). A similar need for a formal recognition of her position (for Kate is so lost, she always wants it established where she is) enters into her relationship with Densher. These two are certainly not, as Dr. Leavis claims, ' "in love" in the full common sense of the phrase.'[13] No one so in love would have been as ready as Kate was to go to her father. That she should wilfully have offered herself to her parent indicates how incompletely her relationship with Densher is sustaining her. Not that she will ever give Densher up. Now that her father has rejected her, her relationship with Densher is the one aspect of her restless search for identity she has determined to rely on as settled. This is why she cements her side of the engagement with such extravagant vows: 'And I pledge you— I call God to witness!—every spark of my faith; I give you every drop of my life' (II, Ch. 2). Kate desperately wants to belong to someone or something other than herself and thereby to be relieved of the penalties of self-absorption. Unfortunately for her, Densher in himself is able to offer her solipsism no remedy. His kind of intelligence only confirms the self-protective, diluted respect Kate has for this faculty. She sees it as a container of 'high dim things' (II, Ch. 1). Moreover Densher as a masculine force is too weak to aid Kate in finding a definition of her female self. She is indeed in a circle of hell. Life turns to her, as she feels, 'the face of a striking and distinguished stranger' (I, Ch. 2), because she is so unreciprocating. But then she is so unreciprocating because the world and her acquaintances only return her to her own barrenness.

As 'an angel with a thumping bank account', Milly both charms and tempts Kate, bringing out paradoxically the best and worst in her. In a single exchange with Densher, Kate can speak of Milly, whose dispossession she recognizes as more drastic than her own, with 'a noble compassion', and yet also regard the American girl as 'just such another victim' as she tells Densher he is. In hands other than an angel's Kate, ironically, is convinced Milly's wealth can have absolute, liberating power. Undoubtedly, Milly herself, by her habitual and casual recourse to her fortune, innocently bears some responsibility for Kate's being governed by this conviction. But then Milly, Kate and Densher always do more of the wrong, than the right, things for one another. As in much of James and in much American literature, they cannot find the middle ground, 'the sincerities, the lucidities, the utilities', on which to be mutually accommodating. What Kate recognizes as Milly's 'ferocity of modesty' and 'intensity of pride' (VI, Ch. 4) make Milly suspicious of, and unresponsive to, compassion—noble or not. Indeed Milly tacitly acquiesces to Kate's patronizing her as a 'dove' (V, Ch. 6), because she gains in this identity an exclusive space for her own manoeuvring. If only she had put Kate in her place on this occasion. It might in several ways have brought matters beneficially to a head. Perhaps it would have brought into the open Kate's repressed love for Milly. As it is, Milly's seeming acquiescence in Kate's composition gives the English girl exactly the wrong opportunity. It allows her worst instincts, to which her best are too likely to be subservient, to predominate. Milly, indeed, might have suspected this would be the outcome of her silence. She already knows that Kate is 'rather indifferently, defensively and, as might be said, by habit of anticipation', 'the least bit brutal' (IV, Ch. 2).

Without help Kate is probably incapable of being other than she is. In Densher's case, however, we might come to a harsher conclusion. In his eyes there is 'the potential recognition of ideas', even if 'you would quite have fallen away . . . on the question of the ideas themselves' (II, Ch. 1). Densher has at least the capacity to *begin* to clarify and change his position. But such clarification as he does arrive at repeatedly gives way to consoling theories. At the head of these is his latent conviction that his natural orbit is to be superior to the ways of the world, whether these be other people's ways of making money, or the habits of his fellow tourists in Venice. The snobbery of his 'mere aesthetic instinct' is revealed early in the novel, when he visits Mrs. Lowder's: 'Never, he felt sure, had he seen so many things so unanimously ugly— operatively, ominously so cruel . . . even while he thought of the quick column he might add up, he felt it less easy to laugh at the heavy horrors than to quail before them' (II, Ch. 2). This response to Mrs. Lowder's furniture has been taken much too literally. Again it is an occasion when the consciousness James creates is as much on display as what it perceives. 'The quick column he might add up' betrays Densher's own complicity as a newspaper man in the commercial values he is eager to convince himself are a 'portentous negation of his own world of thought' (II, Ch. 2). Unlike his creator, who does find it easier to laugh at, than to quail before, Mrs. Lowder and her heavy horrors, Densher begins the novel unaware how self-flattering the response of the aesthetic instinct can be. It is a sign of a limited imagination that Densher can too easily feel he has got someone typecast, whether it be Mrs. Lowder, Kate or Milly. So convinced is he of Kate's strength for life, he never suspects how, in her lostness, she is appealing for 'capture' (II, Ch. 1). As for Milly, she initially can be patronized as 'his little New York friend' (VI, Ch. 1), one of his finds from the general range of American girls who 'when, rare case, they had the attraction of Milly, were clearly the easiest people in the world' (VI, Ch. 5).

In reaction, understandably, against the opportunism Lord

Mark sees as pervasive, Densher too easily denigrates materiality as vulgar, coarse, brutal. He aspires from his own lostness to the pure, the transcendent, the sacred. Occasionally, his frustration with Kate does make it seem that he wants a 'natural' response from her, something other than her schemes and more appropriate to lovers. But all he really asks for at such moments is confirmation from Kate that he has enough will left for self-respect—enough, that is, to qualify the strength of hers. Even at its strongest, his force in the relationship is an intermittent spasm. He is after all onanistically entranced by a private theatre of experience, to which the 'mere aesthetic instinct' is all too likely to succumb. After Kate has come to him in his rooms in Venice (an action on her part which, however much it keeps her side of a bargain, is also a surrender), we read that their encounter

> played for him—certainly in this prime of afterglow—the part of a treasure kept at home in safety and sanctity. . . . The door had but to open for him to be with it again and for it to be all there; so intensely there that, as we say, no other act was possible to him than the renewed act, almost the hallucination of intimacy. . . . He remained thus, in his own theatre, in his single person, perpetual orchestra to the ordered drama, the confirmed 'run;' . . . he couldn't for his life, he felt, have opened his door to a third person. (IX, Ch. 1)

Before the actuality of sexual intercourse with Kate, she had been for him, in a world in which other women were 'but books one has already read' (pornography doesn't last), 'a whole library of the unknown, the uncut' (VI, Ch. 4).

What insight into the confusion of sexual roles in confused times James shows with Kate's and Densher's relationship. Kate, seeing herself as 'only vague and cruelly female' (IV, Ch. 2), is all too tempted by Densher's weakness to 'exist' in him (VI, Ch. 4). Such is his habitual 'failure of insistence', she can always dispose of his pleas that they should marry as they are. While Milly is dying, Densher, anxious to be clean of guilt, again pleads to Kate, 'It's *as* I am that you must have me.' His seeming force, however, is the first act in his ready submission:

> When she had come nearer to him, when putting her hand upon him, she made him sink with her, as she leaned to him,

into their old pair of chairs, she prevented irresistibly, she fore-
stalled, the waste of his passion. She had an advantage with his
passion now. (X, Ch. 2)

Because he feels victimized and impotent in his physical and
material life, Densher is very ready to escape into a transcendent relationship with Milly. When he returns from America,
that apparently superior carelessness before the ways of the
world, which had caused him never to mention Kate when he
was visiting Milly in New York, results in his again allowing
himself to become entangled with his American friend. He is
ready to recognize that if Milly 'weren't a bore she'd be a
convenience' (VI, Ch. 1). Four chapters later, it's clear to him
that she might play a more precise role in his life: 'it wouldn't
really have taken much more to make him wonder if he hadn't
before him one of those rare cases of exultation—food for
fiction, food for poetry.' He knows Milly is being deceived, but
feels that to disillusion her would be to strike 'at the root, in
her soul, of a pure pleasure'. He maintains this idealizing
posture, even though he sees plenty of evidence that Milly has
more ordinary things on her mind and regards his visit as a
significant continuation of his attentions in New York. Book
VI, Chapter 5 is indeed crucial for confirming how much the
re-entry of Densher into her life rekindles the volition she had
wanted to repress in Regent's Park. Seeing Densher earlier,
she had been sure she liked him 'as much as ever', and was
disappointed when he determined 'to be, like everyone else,
simplifyingly "kind" to her. . . . She could have dreamed of his
not having *the* view' (V, Ch. 7). Now, when Densher visits her
in Book VI, Chapter V, she is obviously on the look out for any
opportunity to provoke a sign of his interest in herself. On his
asking her if she can promise she will return from her planned
trip abroad (a question Milly has carefully brought him round
to), we read: 'her face fairly lighted at his asking for a promise.'
Later, when Densher, noticing that Milly is about to go out,
says he must not stand in her way: 'What had happened the
next minute was first that she had denied she was going out, so
that he might prolong his stay; and second that she had said
she would go out with pleasure if he would like to drive.' By
the end of the chapter, her warranty that Kate does not care

for Densher is strengthened by the fact that Kate has called while she was preparing to go out and, finding Densher there, left without staying.

The outcome of Densher's visit and the resulting drive with him leaves Milly fondly wondering 'if one nursed a cause tenderly enough, it might produce an effect' (VII, Ch. 2), and Densher clinging to his high and dim conception that his relationship with Milly belongs in a sublime realm, where she can never be hurt by him, nor he blamed by her. Admittedly, Milly's behaviour towards Densher does give grounds to his temptation to see things in this way. She will eventually bequeath Densher money to forestall self-exposure even after death, and during their scenes together she repeatedly relieves him of embarrassment (and thereby gives his idealism its opportunity) as much to save herself as to save him. Even so, she is more open with Densher than she is with Kate. She clearly reveals to Densher her real interest in him. During their penultimate meeting, it is for the sake of what she has been led to believe she might expect from him, that she makes her most passionate affirmation of her capacity for life. In this scene, she unquestionably gives rein to volition, while Densher, for his part, sees that if Milly is charmingly playing for him the role of consoler for his unrequited love for Kate, she is also testing his response to her own claim on him. It's his understanding of what he is involved in, his full self-knowledge, that generates his eventual terror (an emotion Kate is never morally enough alive to feel) and makes him so substantial and culpable a figure. In Venice, he can even half-satirize to himself his conceptions of Milly 'divine in her trust, or at any rate inscrutable in her mercy'. He knows these are, on his part, 'transcendent motions' (IX, Ch. 1). Because they allow the pressure on him to lighten, however, he will go only a short distance with the self-awareness his satire enacts. Even when Lord Mark's revelations have made Milly's condition desperate and Densher understands the 'general conscious fool's paradise' they have all inhabited, the realization leaves him so unchanged and impotent he will not open Milly's final letter to him. His still unchecked aesthetic instinct leaves the reality of this action to Kate, while he comforts himself with further 'transcendent motions'. In his rooms in London, he preserves a 'thought' so precious he will share it with no one. It is the thought, 'kept . . . back like a favourite pang . . . that he should never know what had been in Milly's letter. . . . The part of it missed forever was the turn she would have given her act. This turn had possibilities that, somehow, by wondering about them, his imagination had extraordinarily filled out and refined' (X, Ch. 1).

3

'She wanted from my own lips—so I saw it—the truth. But I was with her for twenty minutes, and she never asked me for it.'

'She never wanted the truth'—Kate had a high headshake. 'She wanted *you*. She would have taken from you what you could give her and been glad of it, even if she had known it false. You might have lied to her from pity, and she have seen you and felt you lie, and yet—since it was all for tenderness—she would have thanked you and blessed you and clung to you but the more. For that was your strength, my dear man—that she loved you with passion.' (X, Ch. 1)

These comments by Densher and Kate about Milly provide an appropriate occasion for a review of all three characters and for a move to a conclusion. In her assessment of Milly, Kate is also saying more than she knows about herself. The truth she is acquainted with (her family fallen, herself a commodity in others' schemes, her father finally crying over the hollowness of it all) must be something *she* 'never wanted'. Her words above surely confess to the 'what you could give' she herself desired from Densher. They indicate also why she was rarely able to have what she needed from him. She had discounted it in advance, believing it false. Her own need to experience passion and love remains frustrated, because she sentimentalizes and prostitutes it. She seems to give it absolute value, but in fact relegates it to a special, untruthful, unrelated world of its own. Thus relegated, even her own love for Milly (also manifest in her words) can be repressed and transformed into that patronage which later in this scene is confident Milly 'has had *all* she wanted'.

How these words make us wince for the American girl! But then, what *did* Milly want? She was possessed by the truth of

106

personal mortality earlier than most of us ever will be. Always she has a penetrating, and at times mischievous, eye for the fictions in which others would clothe her. Nonetheless, Kate is right. Milly could not face with Densher the fact that he was deceiving her. Consequently she acts towards him in their last meeting as if she had no special claim on him. Treating him as a concerned friend, she lets him know that 'If it was somehow for *her* I was still staying, she wished that to end' (X, Ch. 1). Even her bequest to him is an act of policy and not 'an act of love, an expression of forgiveness, and a transcendence of self'.[14] The strong-minded Milly we are especially reminded of in Venice has too much experience of money to believe it a genuine communication of these things. She knows there is only one kind of person's world in which money allegedly has transcendent power—namely, in Eugenio's. He had said to her, 'Pay enough money and leave the rest to *me*' (VII, Ch. 3), but had provided only for an 'impossible romance' (VII, Ch. 4). The bequest to Densher allows the fiction that she has not been humiliated by his deceit, and that all along her only interest in him had been as a friend, consoling and eventually helping him through the financial obstructions to his marriage to Kate. Wilfully, she makes the ideal role her own. As she has said earlier, with black wisdom, 'idealists, in the long run . . . don't feel that they lose' (IV, Ch. 1).

Milly's own hands *are* 'imbued'. She too fosters 'suppressions which were in the interest of every one's good manner, every one's pity, every one's really quite generous ideal'. She too participates in the 'mere aesthetic instinct of mankind'. As it is for the others, the instinct is all she knows of transcendence. Understandably, Densher readily interprets her not asking for the truth in Venice as a revelation of supreme grace. It gives him nearly all the justification he needs to feel 'something had happened to him too beautiful and too sacred to describe. He had been, to his recovered sense, forgiven, dedicated, blessed' (X, Ch. 2). Not all the justification: he can only share the feeling with the sentimental and ever generous Mrs. Lowder who doesn't know the truth. He cannot bear to recognize it with Kate, who does. All he can hope for with Kate is that Milly can be erased from their mutual consciousness and they can be 'as we were'. In reply to this, however, Kate's words (and the novel's final words) are irrefutable: 'We shall never be again as we were!'

Kate is always ready to look all the truth in the face. Yet she is no more saved by her courage than are Milly and Densher by their fear. The three of them remain estranged from 'the sincerities, the lucidities, the utilities . . . that blessedly, as is assumed, *might* be' on which human intercourse and relief from self depend. In the first part of this essay, I referred to James's own campaign on behalf of these things. As I close this chapter, I am aware that it was easier to refer to the campaign than to demonstrate it. If all meanings can be turned over, if even the wish of the Psalmist, echoed in the novel's title, promotes disaster, where are sincerities, lucidities and utilities to be found? In answer to this question, one can only say on James's behalf that to ask it, as *The Wings of the Dove* asks it, *is* his campaign. The significance of his aesthetic instinct and the dimension of his transcendence of self are revealed in his novel's realization of our common needs.

NOTES

1. The numbers in parentheses refer to Books and Chapters in *The Wings of the Dove* and *The Novels and Tales of Henry James* (New York, 1909). The Roman numeral indicates the Book.
2. I derive the expression, 'life larger for taste', from Chapter 3 of *The Spoils of Poynton*. There, Fleda Vetch is convinced her life is larger for her taste.
3. See Psalm 55.
4. The pronouncement can be conveniently found in Roger Gard (ed.), *Henry James: The Critical Heritage* (London, 1968), p. 343.
5. 'The Pervasive Mystery of Style: *The Wings of the Dove*', in John Goode (ed.), *The Air of Reality: New Essays on Henry James* (London, 1972), pp. 244–300.
6. Other contributors to it are: Frederick C. Crews, *The Tragedy of Manners: Moral Drama in the Later Novels of Henry James* (rpt., Hamden, Connecticut, 1971); R. W. B. Lewis, 'The Vision of Grace: James's *The Wings of the Dove*', *Modern Fiction Studies*, 3 (Spring 1957), 33–40; Quentin Anderson, *The American Henry James* (London, 1958); J. A. Ward, *The Imagination of Disaster: Evil in the Fiction of Henry James* (Lincoln, Nebraska, 1961).
7. *The American Henry James*, p. 237.
8. *The Air of Reality*, p. 284.
9. *The Air of Reality*, p. 245.

10. 'The Dream of Being Possessed and Possessing: Henry James's *The Wings of the Dove*', *Massachusetts Review*, 10 (1969), 103–4.
11. *Henry James: The Major Phase* (London, 1946), p. 64.
12. *The American Scene* (London, 1907) p. 110.
13. *The Great Tradition* (London 1948), Chapter 3.
14. *The Imagination of Disaster*, p. 128.

7

The Golden Bowl:
The Labyrinth of
Consciousness

1

With hindsight we can see that the nature of James's development from *Washington Square* to *The Golden Bowl* was already
potential in his essay, 'The Art of Fiction' (1884). *Washington
Square* had come from the author who declares in the essay that
'the air of reality (solidity of specification) seems to me the
supreme virtue of a novel.' By contrast *The Golden Bowl*, in
which for many readers solidity is remarkable only by its
absence, exists embryonically in James's thoughts about the
kind of experience that might go into a novel. 'What kind of
experience', he asked in the essay, 'is intended, and where
does it begin and end? Experience is never limited, and it is
never complete; it is an immense sensibility, a kind of huge
spider-web of the finest silken threads suspended in the chamber of consciousness, and catching every airborne particle in
its tissue.'

There is no doubt that James's commitment to 'solidity of
specification' signalled his ambition to produce novels whose
realism would rival that achieved by the great nineteenth-
century English and European writers. In accordance with
this ambition, he subscribed, as these writers had done, to the
traditional analogy between the novelist and the historian.

The novelist's work, he wrote in 'The Art of Fiction', 'must speak with assurance, with the tone of the historian'. Solidity of specification derived from the novelist's report on, and imitation of, the reality of the world outside the novel. James came to Europe, because Europe in contrast to America offered a dense and varied spectacle which could be engaged in writing and in personal life. He wanted to be saved from what he convinced himself were Hawthorne's limitations. In his book about his compatriot he concluded that Hawthorne had 'none of the apparatus of an historian, and his shadowy standard of portraiture never suggests a rigid standard of accuracy.' By remaining in America, so James goes on to imply, Hawthorne could hardly have avoided these failings. He could not have had the assurance and specificity of a historian, because in America there was little to be a historian about. The material of a Hawthorne novel is shadowy, according to James, because the America engaged by the author has hardly had time to assume substantiality and definition. 'History, as yet,' James tells us, 'has left in the United States but so thin and impalpable a deposit that we very soon touch the hard substratum of nature; and nature itself in the western world, has the peculiarity of seeming rather crude and immature.'[1]

Like all other arguments about the realism of art, James's is circular. What is real within novels is an imitation of what he recognizes to be real outside of them. Nineteenth-century English and European novels derive 'solidity of specification' from a world richly and variedly endowed with this quality. Their authors can share with their readers a confidence as to what is real. Suppose, however, such confidence is impossible because outside the novel, or any other act of invention, no one is sure about what does exist. This absence of a consensus about reality was always a problem for the nineteenth-century American novelist. Hawthorne, despite what James says, had as a matter of fact at least as much of 'the apparatus of an historian' as James himself. He always understood, however, that his history, as in *The Scarlet Letter*, was fabrication. Faced with an America on which the deposit of history had no confirming force, Hawthorne and his major characters were always in search of an author, an authority, an objectivity, outside the self. They feared that the structure of their lives and of all things else could be no more than an invention.

Nor did James himself ever attain in his fiction the assurance he ascribed to the historian. As I have shown in my chapters on *Washington Square* and *The Portrait of a Lady*, he could at best counterfeit this stance. How could he have a confident grip on what is real when, like all his compatriots, he had experienced the invention of nation? Furthermore, as he came to maturity as a novelist, the English and European structures of reality he wanted to imitate were themselves in doubt. Even on the Eastern side of the Atlantic, the meaning of things seemed less the impersonal bequest of history, more a shifting of contrivance.

The outcome for James is manifest in *The Golden Bowl* in the crucial scene in Book Five, Chapter 2, when Maggie walks the terrace at Fawns and gazes first through the windows of the occupied smoking-room and then through the windows of the empty drawing room:

> Spacious and splendid, like a stage again awaiting a drama it was a scene she might people, by the press of her spring, either with serenities and dignities and decencies, or with terrors and shames and ruins, things as ugly as those formless fragments of her golden bowl she was trying so hard to pick up.

With respect to the other characters in the novel Maggie's position at this moment is frankly authorial and reflects her creator's. Immediately, this episode calls to mind James's famous affirmation, in the Preface to *The Portrait of a Lady*, about the number of windows in 'the house of fiction'. That bold pronouncement about the variety and multiplicity of points of view available to a novelist undermines the notion of objectivity. Together with the title, the *Portrait* of a lady, it implies that reality is inseparable from the way it is composed. In Maggie's case, the 'serenities and dignities and decencies' she eventually chooses are not part of an essential, objective order of things, to which she, or any of the other characters, inherently belongs. They are values adopted in a rented house. Like James's determination, recorded in the preface to *What Maisie Knew*, that Maisie 'for satisfaction of the mind . . . would have to be saved', Maggie's eventual conviction that her characters must not be given up expresses nothing more inevitable and authoritative than authorial predilection. As such it is possessed by a sense of the artificiality and inessentiality of all it contrives. Its theses are always haunted by antitheses. The scenario Maggie chooses, for example, relieves her of one source of nightmare ('terrors and shames and ruins') only to present her with others: her vision that her father is 'holding in one of his pocketed hands the end of a long silken halter looped round [Charlotte's] beautiful neck' (V, Ch. 4)[2]; her 'pity and dread', in the novel's final lines, of the light in her husband's eyes. It is as if there is hardly any firm ground on which to establish those solidities of specification which (be they good or bad) provide for the confirmation of our status. How much, after all, we long to assert, in Eliot's words from 'Burnt Norton', *there* we have been.'

In this instance, Eliot is speaking of the experience of divine redemption from subjectivity, when the absolute is revealed. In *The Golden Bowl*, however, the characters have no communion with authority. Solidities of specification are diffused in 'the chamber of consciousness'. A single sentence from the Preface equates 'an active sense of life' with 'the whole labyrinth of consciousness'. Even after nearly thirty years, Dr. Leavis's response to James's entry into, and presentation of, this labyrinth has classic status. Dr. Leavis regretted James did not go further with what was achieved in *Washington Square*, *The Portrait of a Lady* and *The Bostonians*. All three, as Leavis saw them, had 'the abundant, full-blooded life of well-nourished organisms'. In *The Ambassadors*, *The Wings of the Dove* and *The Golden Bowl*, by contrast, James 'lost his full sense of life and let his moral taste slip into abeyance'. This development had to do with

> certain limiting characteristics of his genius. It was not the explorer's or the pioneer's, and it had nothing prophetic about it. . . . It was not, in short, D. H. Lawrence's or anything like it. James had no such immediate sense of human solidarity, no such nourishing intuition of the unity of life, as could make up to him for the deficiencies of civilized intercourse: life for him must be humane or it was nothing.

There are times when Leavis's criticism of James speaks powerfully to me. I have myself resources for personal and communal fulfilment such as James does not account for. But whether or not these endowments amount to a 'nourishing intuition of the unity of life' is a more open question than Leavis allows. In his account of James, there is an implicit equation between a well-nourished organism and a healthily moral one. The undernourishment of *The Golden Bowl* and its consequent moral sickness are both exemplified in James's calling for a sympathy with Maggie and her father such as we are not ready to give:

> if our sympathies are anywhere they are with Charlotte and (a little) the Prince, who represent what, against the general moral background of the book, can only strike us as a decent passion; in a stale, sickly, and oppressive atmosphere they represent life. That in our feelings about the Ververs there would be any element of distaste Henry James . . . seems to have no inkling.[3]

But what vital claim can be made for Charlotte's and Amerigo's mutual passion when it is incapable of transcending a comparative shortage of money? Surely the point made by their relationship is that their passion only lives parasitically. Incapable of achieving a meaning in itself, it derives a context and sustenance only from the marriage institution it violates. Like their creator, and the other characters in the novel, Charlotte and Amerigo are living in a terminal world. Forms of life they have inherited or adopted are played out. New forms are unperceivable. I am reminded of questions James asked of America in *The American Scene*. 'Do certain impressions there', he wonders, 'represent the absolute extinction of old sensibilities, or do they represent only new forms of them? The inquiry would be doubtless easier to answer if so many of these feelings were not mainly known to us just *by* their attendant forms.'[4] In other words, change the form and you may change the sensibility or feelings, or even, despite Leavis, the 'full sense of life' and 'moral taste'. We are back to the problem of choosing a window in the house of fiction. James would be a greater novelist without 'certain limiting characteristics of his genius'. What significance the missing ingredients would have, however, cannot be guaranteed.

In *The Golden Bowl*, we see fundamental conflicts around which manners and forms of life are revealed as affectation.

For example, 'the insolence of the Empire' (I, Ch. 1), on which Great Britain depends, and amid the structures of which James had hoped to find an objective place, is declared by this phrase alone to be an imposition of meaning, having no justification beyond itself. In response to the disintegration of beliefs, we might say, with the preacher from *Ecclesiastes*, 'the golden bowl is broken'.[5] But in the world of *The Golden Bowl* (a world emphatically without religious resources) we have no right to this lament. Whereas the preacher's words in *Ecclesiastes* refer to a Creator who is God, in *The Golden Bowl* they invoke no authority. In the novel, the golden bowl, product of a 'lost art' (I, Ch. 6), and fortuitously rescued from oblivion, is a haphazardly exploited omen and symbol. It is part of a terminal culture in which objects and texts are losing reference. One thinks of the objects, 'massive and lumpish . . . applied to a hundred uses and abuses', seen 'tumbled together' (I, Ch. 1) in the windows of Bond Street shops. As for texts, they are given an entirely personal reading, such as Adam Verver gives Keats's Sonnet; or, in the case of the history of Amerigo's family shelved in the British Museum, no longer tell their inheritor a sustaining story. Adam Verver builds his 'museum of museums' as 'a house on a rock' of what he believes is absolute taste precisely to redeem himself and America from his prevailing sense that modern life exists on shifting sands. The museum, where great art from the past will be enshrined, is intended by him as an impregnable ark of enlightenment against the unfathomable future the novel itself portends.

If Maggie, gazing through the windows of a 'house of fiction', is one surrogate for James, Adam, devoting his life to art, might be seen as another. Yet, Leavis notwithstanding, James is capable of a critical placing of Adam. Sterility and death follow in Adam's wake, whereas, in the Preface to the novel, James defines the taste of the artist as 'his active sense of life'. Adam's interest in art belongs entirely to the art of the past. It is regressive, wanting to maintain a secure paradise of gilt-edged values. James, however, no mere collector or critic, always faced new frontiers. In this connection, it is significant that in the Preface of this, his last completed novel, he should comment on the opportunity, presented by the *New York Edition*, for the revision of his work. Not surprisingly, he tells us that he finds little revision called for as he re-reads recent productions: 'the march of my present attention coincides sufficiently with the march of my original expression.' But to re-explore his earlier books was to discover the original paths had all but disappeared:

> It was . . . as if the clear matter being still there, even as a shining expanse of snow spread over a plain, my exploring tread . . . had quite unlearned the old pace and found itself naturally falling into another, which might sometimes indeed more or less agree with the original tracks, but might most often, or very nearly, break the surface in other places.

Such an inescapable confronting of blankness reminds us of several famous *loci* in American literature: the ending of *Arthur Gordon Pym* (actually alluded to in *The Golden Bowl*), the prairie in Cooper, the sea and the white whale in Melville. It also causes us to question the certainty of Leavis's denying James the explorer's and pioneer's genius. Genius of this kind need not reach the firm destinations Leavis was demanding of novels. In James's case, it was Adamic in a different sense from in Adam Verver's. It was not regressive and tenacious of security, but strikingly nomadic and experimental. James faced life as Maggie and Amerigo must face it at the end of *The Golden Bowl*. The world all before them, they inhabit it in the name of nothing but what their own relationship will engender. So James lived for nothing that transcended his intercourse with the reader. Across the blank page, mutuality might be established. *There*, with the characters, he and we might be.

Another way of putting it is to say that, in late James especially, we ourselves are involved in the fictional process in which he presents character, and in which characters present themselves to themselves and to their world. This involvement is not simply a matter of our identifying with, or turning from, what is objectively created. Rather, we participate in the act of creation, experiencing the labyrinths and *impasses* of any approach to reality. A possible response to this experience is to discuss James in terms of the strategies of language he employs. My own predilection is to present the results of my participation in the novel. In what follows, I shall offer the results of my reading of Amerigo, Adam, Charlotte and Maggie. On them are focused James's culminating thoughts about America and Europe. Such is his possession of them, such their lack of outward life, it can seem the whole novel is only happening inside the labyrinth of the author's own consciousness. Yet if the characters were too individualized, too emphatically differentiated, it might undermine the effect James intends. As he says in the Preface to 'Lady Barbarina', *The Golden Bowl* presents 'a new scale of relations altogether'. Its subject could 'have been perfectly expressed had *all* the persons concerned been only American or only English or only Roman or whatever', because each character is also its counterpart. We are not to feel that any one state of being is peculiar to the individuality of any one character. As James contemplates in *The Golden Bowl* the culmination of his world, Amerigo, Adam, Charlotte and Maggie become labels for positions any might occupy. This final realization of a mutuality always insistent in James is emphasized in *The Golden Bowl* by the interchanging partnerships. Life has no essential structure, no essential 'solidity of specification', which absolves us from any fate. This is 'the new scale of relations altogether'.

2

We begin the novel contemplating Amerigo's position. He is contemplating it too. If he is not a character projected by the authors of his family's history, who is he? When we first meet him, he is a man so lost to himself, so over-cultured, he has different European languages for different versions of himself. His anxious search for a new author for his life is apparent in his attempt to make Mrs. Assingham responsible for his engagement:

> 'You had the conception.'
> 'Ah, Prince, so had you!'
> He looked at her harder a moment. 'You had it first. You had it most.' (I, Ch. 2)

No longer sustained by his European past, Amerigo is looking (as has much of Europe before and after him) to the American future. In this prospect, however, he is unable to discover any inherent meaning:

He remembered to have read as a boy a wonderful tale by Allan Poe, his prospective wife's countryman ... the story of the shipwrecked Gordon Pym, who drifting in a small boat further toward the North Pole—or was it the South?—than anyone had ever done, found at a given moment before him a thickness of white air that was like a dazzling curtain of light, concealing as darkness conceals, yet of the colour of milk or of snow. There were moments when he felt his own boat move upon some such mystery. The state of mind of his new friends ... had resemblances to a great white curtain. He had never known curtains but as purple even to blackness. (I, Ch. 1)

Amerigo contemplates in his marriage a future apparently unmarked by signposts from the past. Again we see in James how the exhaustion of European ideas of order places Europeans in a position long familiar to Americans. The territory ahead is as blank for Amerigo composing his life as it is for James composing novels which are the analogue of his life. For Amerigo it is a prospect that at one level is revitalizing. It relieves the oppression he feels as someone 'somehow full of his race', full of 'the history, the doings, the marriages, the crimes, the follies, the boundless *betises* of other people'. To escape this past, so the novel's first chapter further reveals, he wants from Maggie 'some new history that should, so far as possible, contradict, and even if need be flatly dishonour, the old'. He wants from her a new moral identity, as much as a new identity in the age of 'vast modern machineries and facilities whose acquaintance he had still to make'. His forthcoming marriage seems to proffer him a new self. Behind the white curtain it seems is redemption from the past. The wealth of America re-establishes a paradise of 'innocent pleasures, pleasures without penalties. [The Ververs'] enjoyment was a tribute to others without being a loss to themselves.'

At another level, however, the tribute the Ververs pay to himself causes Amerigo to question the complacence of both their innocence and also their enjoyment. Without appreciating how her words demean him, Maggie tells Amerigo: 'What was it . . . that made me originally think of you? It wasn't . . . what you call your unknown quality, your particular self. It was the generations behind you.' No wonder Amerigo recognizes, with an inward wince, that in this most serious personal venture for him, 'futility would have been forgiven him. Even *with* it . . . he would have been good enough.' While he, as a European, knows history can be nightmare, his bride-to-be is determined to see it as romance. The Ververs want to possess him only as another piece of guaranteed meaning from the Old World. What Amerigo must be *personally* to be worth what he knows he has cost is a problem which he cannot solve and which the Ververs, in their state of self-congratulation, do not bother to consider. 'Who but a billionaire', Amerigo asks himself with wonderment, 'could say what was fair exchange for a billion?' (I, Ch. 1). Who indeed!

'I see nothing but *you*' are Amerigo's final words to Maggie at the end of the novel. We are told that the statement strangely 'lighted his eyes', and we may find in his words cause for optimism. Amerigo has long needed to see Maggie for herself, just as she has needed to see him for himself. Perhaps at the end, Amerigo and Maggie are about to discover an objectivity in each other. Sexual intercourse, which the closing lines of the novel promise, is one relationship with otherness when our deeply private subjectivity seems to find objective fulfilment. It is one adventure wherein we may escape the 'labyrinth of consciousness'. Yet we do wonder in the name of what Amerigo and Maggie will continue to live their lives. For each to see nothing but the other may eventually become a burden neither can stand. Nor can Amerigo be anything but saddened that Maggie should have learned what he had wanted to unlearn with her: 'Everything's terrible . . . in the heart of man' (VI, Ch. 2). Maggie, leading a life of which Charlotte is the victim, has become as veritable a princess with a corrupting history as any Amerigo might have found on his own side of the Atlantic. His new story for himself may, after all, be the re-writing of an old one. The 'great white curtains of his future' may be as the 'curtains . . . purple even to blackness' of his past.

Such conclusions point to the circularity of the novel. In its turn the circularity accounts for the novel's stillness. James is contemplating representative positions, not presenting the movements and manners of life. It is as if the four main characters are engraved equidistantly on the golden bowl of life. To turn the bowl is to bring one character where another has already been. While Amerigo begins the novel looking from the Old World to the New, Adam Verver is already looking from the New to the Old. The American future has already left Adam unprovided for. For this reason he wants to possess, through his daughter, a prince. Up until 'the sudden hour that had transformed his life', Adam's career as described in Book Second, Chapter 1, had been a triumphant expression of New World energies. He had achieved dominance in the length and breadth of America, but had eventually arrived at 'his Pacific' feeling as unfulfilled as Whitman in the poem, 'Facing West from California's Shores'. He had pioneered the space of America and arrived nowhere. His transformation was his perception then that still 'a world was left to him to conquer'. At last, it seems he has found for his life a transcendent design that will not fail:

> He was happier, doubtless, than he deserved; but *that*, when one was happy at all, it was easy to be. He had wrought by devious ways, but he had reached the place, and what would ever have been straighter in any man's life than his way henceforth of occupying it? It hadn't merely, his plan, all the sanctions of civilization; it was positively civilisation condensed, concrete, consummate, set down by his hands as a house on a rock—a house from whose open doors and windows, open to grateful, to thirsty millions, the higher, the highest knowledge would shine out to bless the land. In this house, designed as a gift primarily to the people of his adoptive city and native State, the urgency of whose release from the bondage of ugliness he was in a position to measure—in this museum of museums, a palace of art which was to show for compact as a Greek temple was compact, a receptacle of treasures sifted to positive sanctity, his spirit to-day almost altogether lived, making up, as he would have said, for lost time and haunting the portico in anticipation of the final rites. (II, Ch. 2)

How perverse it must seem to Adam not to believe his new destiny is manifest and even blessedly pre-ordained! If the experience of great art is a benefit to mankind (and which of us does not believe this?), why should quantities of it not be bought up and access provided to it in a museum in American City? If Americans are not to be Huck Finns (taking 'no stock in dead people'), how else but in a condensed way are they to experience the great civilizations of history? How will they structure the future, if ignorant of the collective past? Such questions in support of Adam, however, lead also to others that count against him. Will not 'civilisation condensed', wrenched from its time and place, be civilization dead and ready indeed for 'final rites'? Ominously, impotence and death do follow in the wake of Adam Verver's 'monomania' (II, Ch. 6), as in the wake of Captain Ahab's. Remembering his first wife, he thinks: 'they had loved each other so that his own intelligence, in the higher line, had temporarily paid for it.' Now he cannot resist seeing it as necessary to his destiny that his wife's influence should have been 'so promptly removed' (II, Ch. 1) by her early demise. No wonder the inhabitants of American City feel the need to protect themselves, by jibing at Adam, from the godlike eminence he wishes to claim for himself in their community.

'It was all, at bottom, to him, the aesthetic principle' (II, Ch. 5). In making this diagnosis of Adam, James is again asking, as in previous novels, to what extent anyone's life is larger for this principle. How far can we believe in Adam's insidious, exhilarating presumption that, having attained the appreciative heights of a connoisseur, we don't 'after all per-haps dangle so far below the great producers and creators'? If we so dangle, what rewards for ourselves and mankind at large are reserved for our dangling? How *is* the appreciation of any work of art (such as Keats's sonnet on Chapman's Homer, which means so much to Adam) to be 'fitted . . . to a fact of experience' (II, Ch. 1)? In an age when the aesthetic principle can, on the one hand, seem to be the only access to transcen-dence, but, on the other, can be recognized, in Merton Densher's words from *The Wings of the Dove*, as 'the mere aesthetic instinct of mankind', such questions justifiably com-pel James's attention. In Keats's sonnet on Chapman's Homer, there is no conflict between the life of the imagination and life in the material sense. Discovery in art and discovery in the material world are the product of analogous energies commanding equal appreciation. The poet and Cortes are as one. By the end of the nineteenth century, however, this equation no longer holds. Adam Verver has 'wrought by devious ways'. He knows, in the words of Conrad's Marlowe, that 'the conquest of the earth . . . is not a pretty thing when you look into it too much.'[6] In compensation for this guilt, life and art are separated, the former being subordinated to what appear as the supreme, inviolable claims of the latter. But Adam has paid dearly, in human terms, for his monomania. He has lost touch with life's everyday intimacies and reciprocities. So demanding is his taste, every birthday gift to him is a 'foredoomed abberation', even if 'cherished' (IV, Ch. 9). So incapable is he of coping with the ordinary human event, when we first meet him he is in flight (comically for us) from Mrs. Rance. He is always young for Maggie, but may alternatively be seen as a 'small spare slightly stale person' (II, Ch. 4). Perhaps Charlotte is right in her claim that it is he who in their marriage is impotent.

The questions raised by Adam's fixed commitment to the aesthetic principle are not exclusively the product of his Americanness. Nonetheless, James conceives Adam as representative, in Maggie's words, of 'the American way' (I, Ch. 1). As in the case of the idealism of Emerson, Whitman and Melville's Captain Ahab, Adam's search is always for the absolute. So boundless seem the opportunities of being American, no compromise must be settled for. The end must match the promise of the beginning. The scale of life must always be major. Adam, therefore, gives complete allegiance to what appear to him to be transforming moments of vision. As he holds 'his breath with wonder' (II, Ch. 5), when he realizes he must marry Charlotte, he is like Gatsby, the later idealist, with Daisy. In Emerson's words, 'all mean egotism vanishes'[7] from his design at such moments. Yet there remains a culpably sublime egotism, a culpably sublime narcissism, about him. As Amerigo, Charlotte and Maggie discover, Adam will not relate to the world on terms other than those deriving from his grand visions. In what Maggie recognizes as his 'secret unrest' (V, Ch. 3), he is too conscious that without his design he himself, *personally*, is a hollow man. Were other American visions, we wonder, similarly the product of an inevitable personal diminishment before the immensity of space to be filled? Adam remains impervious, even wilfully so, to the darker implication of what he is doing. Presumably, he questioned no further how his money was made, in what Twain labelled 'the Gilded Age', than he questions now his scheme 'to rifle the Golden Isles' of their art (II, Ch. 1). How blind he remains to what Charlotte must think about the terms on which he offers her marriage, and in which he accounts to her for Maggie's marriage to Amerigo. What a dilemma Charlotte is placed in by his proposal. Given her circumstances, she is in response as honourable as anyone could expect her to be, and certainly as honourable as Adam lets her be. We are touched by his joy when Charlotte accepts him. But, in his need to be 'made . . . right' (II, Ch. 7), there is so little Adam allows himself to be told.

Charlotte too wants to be made right. In her case, however, the need is not accompanied by any sense of mission. It amounts rather to a longing for accommodation and context. Of the four main characters, Charlotte is the one to whom we have the least direct access. We very rarely enter her consciousness. These facts, together with Maggie's sense of Charlotte's eventual fate, can make it seem that Charlotte is not given her just deserts even by her creator. We might feel that not even James allows Charlotte what George Eliot terms 'an equivalent centre of self'. George Eliot speaks of our apprehending this centre in others as 'an idea wrought back to the directness of sense, like the solidity of objects'.[8] In other words, there is for George Eliot a centre to people as solid as the solidity of the material world. This belief is the bed-rock of her understanding of character. It means she can present character with remarkable firmness of specification. She knows how her characters work. She knows, in all her humanity, where on the solid scale of things their moral responsibility lies.

But what about characters whose centre of self is so unreachable, either by others or by themselves, as to discredit confidence in the notion of its existence? That this dispossession may be Charlotte's plight begins to be apparent from the moment she enters the novel:

> She could have looked at [Mrs. Assingham] with such straightness and brightness only from knowing that the Prince was also there—the discrimination of but a moment, yet which let him take her in still better than if she had instantly faced him. . . .

123

He knew her narrow hands, he knew her long fingers and the shape and colour of her finger-nails, he knew her special beauty of movement and line when she turned her back, and the perfect working of all her main attachments, that of some wonderful finished instrument, something intently made for exhibition, for a prize. He knew above all the extraordinary fineness of her flexible waist, the stem of an expanded flower, which gave her a likeness also to some long loose silk purse, well filled with gold pieces, but having been passed empty through a finger-ring that held it together. It was as if, before she turned to him, he had weighed the whole thing in his open palm and even heard a little the chink of the metal. When she did turn to him it was to recognise with her eyes what he might have been doing. She made no circumstance of thus coming upon him, save so far as the intelligence in her face could at any moment make a circumstance of almost anything. If when she moved off she looked like a huntress, she looked when she came nearer like his notion, perhaps not wholly correct, of a muse. (I, Ch. 3)

This passage is a paradigm of Charlotte's relationship with the world. In it we see her emptiness to be, irresolvably, both inherent and also a product of the way the world has used her. Her habit of self-display is the strategy of someone wanting to conceal emptiness. To this end, she presents herself as an object for the connoisseur. Mrs. Assingham's denial to her husband notwithstanding, the passage makes it clear Charlotte and Amerigo have been lovers. Yet Charlotte has allowed Amerigo to know her only on the outside.

Belief that one has a centre of self must derive to a significant degree from the conviction that the world accedes to the self. Charlotte never has this conviction. In the above passage we see how Amerigo, whose patronizing of women has already been shown to amount to a latent contempt for them, satisfies himself with Charlotte as with 'some wonderful finished instrument'. His and the world's exploitation of Charlotte, as a cluster of 'attachments' has confirmed her self-perversion and self-prostitution. Now the value of her every motion is calculated in her own eyes and in her beholder's. As a 'huntress', she searches for accommodation, context, connection. Wherever and whenever they are found, she can then, as a 'muse', create a role. It is a performance which must finally unnerve most spectators, since it undermines faith in integrity and sincerity. Presumably Charlotte, who *is* a prize, has never married, because no one had sufficient belief in his own centre of self to withstand her loss of belief in hers. Only Adam can call on enough egotism for two people.

To play a part is one reason Charlotte has come back to Amerigo so immediately before his marriage. So much is evident from their scene together in Book Second, Chapter 5, as they begin their search for a present for Maggie. The insistence in Charlotte's accounting for the occasion, prefaced by her exclamation that she wants to be 'absolutely honest' and doesn't 'want to pretend', betrays someone desperately trying to convince herself of the sincerity of what she says. Perhaps Charlotte would like to play as 'heroic' and 'sublime' a part on Amerigo's and Maggie's behalf as Mrs. Assingham had imagined for her in the previous chapter. Perhaps she would like to believe she too can be a Maggie Verver and give herself away, as she tells Amerigo, 'for nothing'. At the same time, we should remember that Charlotte has just returned from America, where she found nothing. With this knowledge the scene, as it develops, becomes her last attempt to win Amerigo for herself. In this respect, the passion in her voice is genuine, though she misrepresents it by her words. If Amerigo had given Charlotte the response she wants on this occasion, it might have been better for her. But even when she finds the nearest thing she has to a real desire, it is unreciprocated. Amerigo pays no homage to their past relationship. Determinedly listening only to Charlotte's words, 'he clutched . . . at what he could best clutch at—the fact that she let him off, definitely let him off.' It is an unresponsiveness on Amerigo's part which leaves Charlotte only with the energy of despair. As the scene ends, we listen to her trying to darken Amerigo's future in what she, with Mrs. Assingham, must see as 'the Golden Isles' (I, Ch. 2). Desolate herself, she would like to drive a wedge between Amerigo and Maggie. We read that in her references to Maggie she 'might have been talking . . . of someone with whom he was comparatively unconnected'. She changes her statement, 'If you love her', to 'I should say, if she loves you', and is quick to seize on possible criticisms of Maggie: for example, 'She's not selfish—God forgive her!—

enough.' If only she could get Amerigo to believe that to be soiled like himself and herself is a more human condition than Maggie's, what a consolation it would be.

All readers of *The Golden Bowl* feel uneasy about Charlotte's fate as it is seen by Maggie. Yet we do not know that Charlotte herself interprets her marriage in Maggie's stark terms. We do not know that she feels her neck to be in a noose held by her husband. We infer she must feel victimized by life, but conclude also her marriage must provide recompense. As she tells Adam when he proposes, she has long sought 'a motive for one thing more than another—a motive outside of myself' (II, Ch. 6). This motive her marriage will continue to give her, even if she is in despair over her absolute separation from Amerigo. If, put at the worst, her marriage is an enslavement to the will of an impotent old man, it is also, put at the best, the complete worldly accommodation she needs. All it requires is that she play a part, and who is better equipped than she to do this? She has long lost contact with any real self. Even her adultery was a performance. Does she not then eventually settle for her role as Adam's wife? She is, we must remember, an original author of Maggie's and Amerigo's marriage. Her presence when they first became acquainted would have prevented the marriage. Later, any word about her earlier relationship with Amerigo would destroy the Verver's arrangements. Her compliance, therefore, in the eventual scheme of things is also an assertion of status and even a negative expression of power. Certainly, Maggie feels Charlotte's power. She becomes aware of Charlotte's tacit demand that '[Charlotte] must remain safe and Maggie must pay—what she was to pay with being her own affair' (V, Ch. 2).

To belong in a system, even as victim or loser, is better than not to belong anywhere and be nothing. It is as well this is the case, since neither the systems of the world nor the systems of works of art (not even George Eliot's) ever grant everyone an 'equivalent centre of self'. They all demand someone should accept with Prufrock 'I am not Prince Hamlet, nor was meant to be.' Charlotte, finally, is the loser anyone might be in a given system. This is why she is presented by James from the outside, as someone to whom systems are applied. In the Ververs' house of fiction, and seen through Maggie's window, Charlotte is the loser who defines Maggie as winner and who therefore, Maggie guiltily recognizes, is 'necessary' (VI, Ch. 2) *as* loser. What Charlotte is through her own window we never know, and that is James's point. Her own window may be another system, another novel, the possibility of which admits the partiality of the structures presented in *The Golden Bowl.*

In other words, even though Book Second of the novel is devoted almost exclusively to the structure of Maggie's experience, her point of view is not presented as absolute by James. Maggie's is the 'labyrinth of consciousness' in which James has most interest in *The Golden Bowl.* Nevertheless, hers is another of the many consciousnesses James has exhibited for our sympathetic, critical attention. From the beginning, Maggie is unfulfilled by the paradise her father has contrived. Unlike Adam, she has not reached the gardens at Fawns after having 'wrought by devious ways'. The happiness commanded by her father's wealth can rob her life of motive and discount achievement—even that of her marriage. In Book Second, Chapter 4, in the first of the intermittent assessments of their position which always confess the Ververs' unease, she tells her father: 'I might easily be ridiculous . . . by behaving as if I thought I had done a great thing.' To avoid ridicule, and to pre-empt what could be seen as the self-indulgence of discontent (what *is* to be settled for if Fawns is not to be settled for?), Maggie has become, in her own words, 'a small creeping thing'. Perhaps more wilfully than Jane Austen's Fanny Price or than Dickens's Little Dorrit, she has concluded 'one can always for safety be kind.' Meanwhile, she lives vicariously in Charlotte. She tells her father:

> 'She hasn't a creature in the world really—that is nearly—belonging to her. Only acquaintances who, in all sorts of ways, make use of her, and distant relations who are so afraid she'll make use of *them* that they seldom let her look at them.'
> Mr Ver ver was struck—and, as usual, to some purpose, 'If we get her here to improve *us* don't we too then make use of her?'
> It pulled the Princess up, however, but an instant. 'We're old, old friends—we do her good too. I should always, even at the worst—speaking for myself—admire her still more than I used her.'
> 'I see. That always does good.'

Maggie seemed to consider his way of putting it. 'Certainly—she knows it. She knows, I mean, how great I think her courage and her cleverness. She's not afraid—not of anything; and yet she no more ever takes a liberty with you than if she trembled for her life. . . . I never saw her do anything but laugh at her poverty.'

This discussion of Charlotte reveals again in James the extent to which he observed human relationships to be inescapably a matter of mutual exploitation. Remaining systems of manners mask the exploitation, but they hardly redeem it. Adam, as indicated by his responses to Maggie, shares the view of his creator in this respect. It is another reason for his trying to secure himself by renting Fawns, a great English house where one might still be convinced of the graciousness of life. This act, like Mr. Touchett's purchase of Gardencourt in *The Portrait of a Lady*, is analogous to James's own early attempts to secure himself as a novelist by adopting a voice of European urbanity. Adam's responses to Maggie confirm that his apparent imperviousness to doubt on other occasions is as deliberate as the unchanging uniform of his clothes. Despite Maggie's confidence, it is doubtful if Charlotte laughs at her poverty when Maggie is not looking, and she must wish she did not always have to call on courage and cleverness. Maggie's confidence about what 'does good' is itself an affectation. If it were not, she would not be so fearful of life. She would not live parasitically on Charlotte's courage. Like Little Dorrit's, Maggie's excessive filial consideration for her father is also her own fear (not unjustified) of what awaits in the adult world. If at the heart of all are the barren lies of Mrs. Assingham, why not remain uncorrupted in Adam's harmonious domain? Maggie's assurances to her father that he is young imply that she herself remains even younger. Safe in Adam's paradise, she is as if eternally virgin even after her marriage. For his part, Adam too is content. When he proposed to Charlotte, he affirmed his desire for a wife with the protest: 'Can't a man . . . be anything but a father?' (II, Ch. 6). Yet he derives more consolation from intimacy with flesh of his flesh than from intercourse with the otherness represented by Charlotte. With Maggie, he is indeed as the unfallen Adam in the garden. Everything is part of him, and he is part of everything.

128

Such is the 'arrangement' which, at the very beginning of Book Fourth, presents itself to Maggie's consciousness 'like some strange tall tower of ivory, or perhaps rather some wonderful beautiful but outlandish pagoda'. As Maggie puts it to herself:

> The pagoda in her blooming garden figured the arrangement— how otherwise was it to be named?—by which, so strikingly, she had been able to marry without breaking, as she liked to put it, with her past. She had surrendered herself to her husband without the shadow of a reserve or a condition and yet hadn't all the while given up her father by the least little inch.

To some extent this reflection is valedictory. Maggie has already started to break with her past in the difference she has made to the 'arrangement'. She did not wait at her father's for Amerigo's return with Charlotte. Instead she came home alone, so that Amerigo would find her there. This move may signal an embryonic awareness of her earlier self-deception: in not giving up her father, she had not surrendered herself to her husband.

In the second half of the novel we participate in Maggie's transforming herself from a Fanny Price or a Little Dorrit, someone who suspects she may not even be interesting to others, into a Jane Eyre, someone 'no longer playing with blunt and idle tools, with weapons that didn't cut' (IV, Ch. 1). Yet James does not claim, as Charlotte Brontë does with Jane, that one can ever be the complete reader of one's own experience. We read all of James's characters better than they read themselves. It is as if objectivity about the self, even in self-examination, may only ever be conferred by a putative reader of the self. Maggie is aware of something of her own part in what happened. She knows that it 'came from her not having been able not to mind—not to mind what became of [her father]. . . . She had made anxiety her stupid little idol' (IV, Ch. 4). Her father, however, has needed her anxiety on his behalf. So much is made clear in their assessments of their lives in Book Fourth, Chapter 5 and in Book Fifth, Chapter 3. On both these occasions, the possible hollowness of Adam's achievement trembles on the brink of explicit mutual recognition. Maggie perceives on the first occasion that her father is 'terrified' that what he calls 'my old show' might be even more fundamentally called into question than his own terminology allows for. On the second, she eventually responds to her sense of his 'secret unrest' with the words: 'I believe in you more than any one.'

No sympathetic reader of these two scenes could ever feel it humane that Adam should have the curtain of his 'old show' brought down by any action of Maggie's. At the same time her patronizing of him has implications she does not recognize. It is an unnatural inversion of their relationship, causing her at one stage to liken the old man to the 'doll' she had as a 'little girl' (IV, Ch. 4). Her confessed desire 'to possess and use' (IV, Ch. 3) Amerigo and Charlotte extends, we see, to her father. Maggie, ruling the world of the other three, is at last significant in her own eyes. In this connection her belief in Adam is necessary for self-belief. As her father, he does of course predicate her, but it is more than this. Like Nick Carraway's penultimate words to Gatsby ('You're worth the whole damn bunch put together'), Maggie's belief in her father encloses him in a structure of meaning within which she too can maintain a hold on things.

She is after all threatened, or, in her own word which heightens the drama of her position, *'menaced'* (IV, Ch. 4). As Gabriel Pearson has shown, in an outstandingly intelligent essay,[9] the tower of ivory and the pagoda appearing in the garden of her life represent experience Maggie had consented to be excluded from. The structures clearly may have sexual implications; the tower, the phallus; the pagoda, the womb. Maggie, cloistered with her father, has caused Amerigo and Charlotte to do her sexual living for her. Her life has been too undisturbed by energies suggested by the tower and the pagoda. She has been too untroubled by what her father's *imperium* has repressed. In this context, the tower of ivory and the pagoda have a Conradian dimension. They hint at ways of life vanquished by the insolence of any empire, so that its own 'serenities and decencies and dignities' can be preserved. With the appearance of the tower of ivory and the pagoda, we are experiencing Maggie's intimation that every thesis has its pressing antithesis. All values (including those of the aesthetic principle) may be no more than the self-justification of particular desires and acts of power. They may also be no more than impositions on the void. How comforting it would be if entry into the strange structures in the garden could be read as a fall into the knowledge of good and evil. This reading, however, would give a moral firmness to Maggie's development such as the novel does not finally sponsor. The tower of ivory may be no less blank, the pagoda no less hollow, than the garden Maggie feels she must leave, or than the snow-plain across which James constructed his prose. On Adam Verver's part, 'the constant flawless freshness of the white waistcoat', while it proclaims that he is unsoiled, also betrays his own intimacy with blankness and the void. I am thinking of this moment, when he is witnessed by Maggie as he sits by her sleeping son:

> her father sat there with as little motion—with head thrown back and supported, with eyes apparently closed, with the fine foot that was so apt to betray nervousness at peace upon the other knee, with the unfathomable heart folded in the constant flawless freshness of the white waistcoat that could always receive in its armholes the firm prehensile thumbs. (V, Ch. 5)

If there is not a void at the heart of things, is there anything other than the atavism of prehensile thumbs? Such questions lurk for Maggie behind doors she would rather not open. Her fear of sexual passion, still evident in her 'dread' at the end, pertains to her suspicion that the 'serenities and decencies and dignities', in which she wishes to preserve her own identity and the identities of the other three, may be no more than a veneer. To concede too far to whatever is natural may be to break through the veneer and lose all bearings. How far, to adopt the terminology of *Death in Venice*, dare one go 'to the tigers'?[10] As Maggie looks in through the windows of Fawns on her three relatives, she is tempted to make a passionate exposure, but finally sees this temptation as a 'provocation of opportunity which had assaulted her . . . as a beast might have leaped at her throat' (V, Ch. 2). That way lay a self-destruction from which there may have been no rebirth. Not to have taken it will remain a loss for Maggie such as she may not appreciate. Her dread feeds on her determination to remain self-possessed. In its turn, her determination to remain self-possessed makes us doubt her conviction that she 'could make love' to Amerigo (IV, Ch. 3). Even so, by resisting the beast, she secures a structure of life necessary as much for the others as herself.

But it is a structure based on lies Maggie allows to pass for truth. How can complicity in such mendacity be other than self-confounding and self-corrupting? As if in implicit answer to these questions, much of Book Second can be read as Maggie's attempt to establish a drama in which real verities, real positions, may be identified. It is vital to Maggie, for example, that Charlotte should be 'tragic', 'doomed to a separation that was like a knife in her heart' (V, Ch. 5). Enclosed in counterfeits, Maggie imposes on Charlotte the truths she needs to believe in. Charlotte, separated from Amerigo, is the embodiment of loss and defeat. She proves, in Maggie's eyes, that there are fundamental passions, the positive of which Maggie has yet to experience. Maggie, therefore, imagining Charlotte to be tapping at a glass as if to reach her, translates the tapping into these words: 'You don't know what it is to have been loved and broken with. You haven't been broken with, because in *your* relation what can there have been worth speaking of to break? (VI, Ch. 1). Maggie is troubled that Amerigo himself bears the break with Charlotte with such resignation. His submission to events calls into question his capacity for real feeling and must, therefore, cast doubt on his feeling for Maggie herself. Even the certainties most needed by Maggie remain insecure.

Her belief in her father 'more than anyone' is shaken when a door in the labyrinth of her consciousness opens to reveal him 'holding in one of his pocketed hands the end of a long silken halter looped round [Charlotte's] beautiful neck'.

> He didn't twitch it, yet it was there; he didn't drag her, but she came; and those betrayals that I have described the Princess as finding irresistible in him were two or three mute facial intimations which his wife's presence didn't prevent his addressing his daughter—nor prevent his daughter, as she passed, it was doubtless to be added, from flushing a little at the receipt of. They amounted perhaps only to a wordless smile, but the smile was the soft shake of the twisted silken rope, and Maggie's translation of it, held in her breast till she got well away, came out only, as if it might have been overheard, when some door

was closed behind her. 'Yes, you see—I lead her now by the neck, I lead her to her doom, and she doesn't so much as know what it is, though she has a fear in her heart which, if you had the chances to apply your ear there that I, as a husband, have, you would hear thump and thump and thump.' (V, Ch. 4)

This episode, in its surrealism and in some of its import, reminds me of the chapter, 'The Whipper', in *The Trial.* Joseph K, opening a door to a room in the bank in which he works, is suddenly confronted with two men being flogged. They are inevitable victims of the status he claims for himself as a human being, even though he never intends anyone should suffer for his sake. Similarly, in the above episode, life tries Maggie beyond her capacity for response. She has found it appropriate that Charlotte be cast as victim. Such casting has even been an expression of her compassion. Yet she has never wanted Charlotte to be a victim to the extent intimated above. She has never understood victimization by the Ververs to be of this order. May it be that her father, in his impotence and in his monomania, is at heart entirely barren of human feeling? Is he only a function of his prehensility? Oh, that the door never opened on these questions.

3

' "See"? I see nothing but *you*.' And the truth of it had with this force after a moment, so strangely lighted his eyes that as for pity and dread of them she buried her own in his breast.

In response to Amerigo's last words, Maggie buries her eyes as one aware there is too much to see. For relief, she turns to pity, the source of which, however, is the very self that dreads what it sees. She turns also to Amerigo, but he, in his turn, is no more endowed, no less impoverished, than the self she turns from. In the name of what will they now continue to live?

Like the novel of which they are part, Maggie and Amerigo face the trial of the twentieth century never having been sustained by solidities and fulfilments formerly available. So unprovided for, it may be they will be too much thrust in on what may prove to be their own insubstantiality. For many readers, *The Golden Bowl* itself is certainly too much thrust in on *its* insubstantiality. What a strange outcome it is that James, who at the outset of his career believed that 'to be an American [was] an excellent preparation for culture',[11] who so generously responded to the productions of other artists, should yet at the end appear so essentially unaccommodated. In this last completed novel, he has no fragments to shore against his ruins; nothing, it seems, to rest on in community with his readers: not a shared place, building, book, painting, piece of music, meal, game—not a prayer. Yet it is in this very state of dispossession that his community with his characters and his readers has its origin. 'Giving them up was, marvellously, not to be thought of' (V, Ch. 2). So it comes to Maggie, as she gazes on the occupants of the room at Fawns. The conviction is also her creator's. Not to share it with James, despite the irredeemable 'split . . . between conviction and action' (IV, Ch. 10) would be final destitution.

NOTES

1. *Hawthorne* (London, 1879), Chapter 1.
2. The numbers in parentheses refer to Books and Chapters in *The Golden Bowl* in *The Novels and Tales of Henry James* (New York, 1909). The Roman numeral indicates the Book.
3. *The Great Tradition* (London, 1948), Chapter 3.
4. *The American Scene* (London, 1907), p. 146.
5. *Ecclesiastes*, XII, 6.
6. *Heart of Darkness*, Chapter 1.
7. See Emerson's *Nature*, Chapter 1.
8. *Middlemarch*, Chapter 21.
9. 'The Novel to end all Novels: *The Golden Bowl*', in John Goode (ed.), *The Air of Reality: New Essays on Henry James* (London, 1972), pp. 301–60.
10. *Death in Venice*, Penguin Books (London, 1955), p. 12.
11. See James's letter of September 1867 to T. S. Perry. It can be found in Roger Gard (ed.), *Henry James: The Critical Heritage* (London and New York, 1968), pp. 22–3.

Index